Achieving SPEM Health
Spiritual Physical Emotional Mental
(It's Up to You!)™

Judith C. Lista

ISBN 979-8-88540-846-2 (paperback)
ISBN 979-8-88540-848-6 (hardcover)
ISBN 979-8-88540-847-9 (digital)

Christian Faith Publishing
832 Park Avenue
Meadville, PA 16335
www.christianfaithpublishing.com

NIV used for all Biblical Scriptures

Printed in the United States of America

CONTENTS

FOREWORD
by, Joseph W. Lista, MS, PA-C

There are many self-help books written by degreed professionals, who are titled in the subject(s) they write about. While they use tried-and-true methods of reaching out to help readers learn and grow, Judith C. Lista has an intuitive talent to write with deep personal truths that reach out to everyday readers' concerns and needs.

The publishing of **Achieving SPEM Health**™ has been Judy's dream for years! Having been together for (18) years (married in 2018), I know that her genuine interest in the **Spiritual, Physical, Emotional, and Mental (SPEM) Health** details of her life is coupled with her sincere desire to share her learnings with people interested in bettering their health and their lives. Judy has a strong belief in people sharing their knowledge with others, which is the basic structure of this book.

People find various ways to help others, but not everyone wishes to spend their time writing manuscripts and working to find publishers. However, Judy loves to write and is extremely interested in putting her honest thoughts on paper to describe her healthy growth in life. You will read helpful ideas in **Achieving SPEM Health**™, which will motivate you to get started on improving your **SPEM Health** and **your life!** She includes meaningful biblical scriptures throughout her writing, which are very encouraging.

Judy's resume has (35+) years of experience in Sales, Marketing, Customer Service, and Public Relations. As an entrepreneur, Judy created and managed (5) small businesses since 1990. She received her Business Degree in her early (40s) while creating and managing a small business, plus, hosting a Live AM Talk Radio Show about Life Issues. While in college, she proudly received the award for, "The Most Outstanding Entrepreneur of the Year." And she recently retired from a nonprofit career as, Coordinator of Volunteers, Development, and Special Events, where her bevy of skills made a remarkable impact!

As I continue to enjoy working for a Family Practice in Central, Pennsylvania, Judy is doing what she has dreamed of for a long time! Working full-time as a non-fiction writer of several manuscripts, and a movie script, as well. Her ability to open the minds and hearts of readers with truths about health and life, is remarkable!

You will enjoy Judy's strong faith in God, and that she is a Survivor not only of life-threatening car accidents, but she is, also, a (2) time breast cancer Survivor!

Judy has an incredible resiliency to get through difficulties. She continues in life with hopes of helping others motivate themselves to learn and grow to become Survivors in various life situations. Enjoy the practical way that she shares why you should look more deeply into your thoughts and actions to start living a healthier, happier life, while growing closer to God! **AMEN**

ACKNOWLEDGMENTS

Thank you, God, for guiding me wisely through small and large experiences in my life. Whether the results were positive or negative, each has brought me to where I am today, stronger in my faith and closer to You every day! Thank you for guiding me so well! **AMEN**

Throughout the years, many friends from church, college, and employment shared biblical scriptures with me that were special in their lives. Thank you for giving me reason to rejoice with your faith in God's Word. You may find your "favorites" within this book! **AMEN**

I would like to thank my husband, Joseph W. Lista, for his belief in me! He has stood strongly beside me during my climb up the non-fiction literary ladder to find success! He means the world to me! Thank you for being in my corner during this wonderful experience in life! Together, we will continue to grow as strong Christian stewards of God's powerful messages! **AMEN**

INTRODUCTION

Do you really, really want to be healthy? Of course you do! Nearly everyone does! This book explores different avenues you can take to achieve and maintain good health. Keep in mind that good health is much more than just physical well-being and it can be found despite serious physical and mental disabilities and infirmities. A healthy person is one whose spirit and inner essence provides a strong grounding and motivation for life. Good health requires that the **PHYSICAL** body, inside and out, from head-to-toe, is treated and well cared for to maximize its capabilities. No matter what health-related issues you have at this moment, it is still important to make the most of what you can have! Plus, one's **EMOTIONAL** thoughts and feelings should be fully experienced yet harnessed to reach positive ends. A healthy person continually develops and employs his or her mind for the benefit of self and of larger society. Good health, therefore, results from being healthy **Spiritually, Physically, Emotionally, and Mentally** which I call **SPEM Health**. Instead of saying, How are you? Let's all start asking ourselves and others, **"How is your SPEM Health?"** Get this important question started with yourself and people in your life!

You probably realize that many people do not give anything more than lip service to improving how they live their lives. Be honest! Does that describe **YOU**? I had a traumatic car accident due to **UNhealthy CHOICES** I made. That was MY TIME to realize, that statement, was ABOUT ME!

This Book Shows That Improvement Starts with Your → A, B, Cs

A—Pay attention to improving your **SPEM Health** as you build a firmer foundation for a healthier life. Do not put it off! Get started today!

B—Adjust different aspects of your thinking and behavior to limit the number of problems that come into your life. You can do it!

C—While admitting there will be ups-and-downs during your effort to improve your **SPEM Health**, forgive yourself for any backslides that occur during your growth process. As you continue on your **SPEM Health Journey**, better days are ahead!

I will say again, no matter what health issues you have now, from head-to-toe, it is still possible to make the most of what **YOU CAN** have. Listen, it is easy to grow tired of the difficulties we face in life. We get stuck in old, hard-to-break habits, which contribute to the lack of **Healthy** growth within our minds and in our actions. And, often, people are born with **SPEM Health** difficulties that they must learn to work around in life.

I hope you will become aware of your inherent strengths and abilities to improve the condition and direction of your life **SOONER** than I did! I know you have heard the phrase, "Better late than never!" I would rather say, "If you start today, it won't be too late, but, if you wait until tomorrow, it might be!" HEY! I almost DIED, and my life changed drastically before I chose to start making needed, **HEALTHY** adjustments, first and foremost, to my thinking!

Making **HEALTHY SPEM** changes is what many lives are lacking and need! People EASILY get help for their **PHYSICAL** Health problems; however, they do NOT EASILY think of getting help for their **EMOTIONAL and MENTAL** Health problems. But, they should! Each part of our **SPEM Health** is equally important for us to stay healthy! Everyone should get a "mental tune-up" during their life, as often as needed through their own efforts, and/or, with a qualified therapist.

This book strongly reflects the need for a **SPIRITUAL** connection to complete the wholeness of all ingredients, which, together, build a truly healthy mind/body/spirit foundation for each of us. I am a Christian who believes in God's will. I find it hard to understand how people, who do not have a **SPIRITUAL** belief system in place, live their lives to the fullest. Where do they go within themselves when they look for answers to difficult experiences that occur in their lives? How do they find solace when faced with the loss of a loved one or deal with their own impending mortality? How are they able to experience full joy in life? Are they able to look at the innocent twinkling of a baby's eye and fully comprehend the miracle of life? Fingerprints and DNA did not just happen by chance! How do nonbelievers go through all the ups-and-downs in life without having a strong faith during all the questions, thoughts, and feelings they have while alive? How do they forgive themselves and others for mistakes they make in life? Why don't they believe in something greater than themselves?

Of course, there is no magic wand that will instantly turn the difficult realities of your life into perfectly healthy ones. Therefore, we must EACH work to improve our **SPEM Health** DAILY. Now, do NOT go overboard and ONLY think about what and how to change and do nothing else. Put everything into a Healthy perspective! By improving the way your mind/body/spirit components work, you will be able to rid yourself of UNhealthy behavioral patterns that have either stymied your growth potential or left you as an unwilling participant in life. So, please, just take ONE day at a time, and **YOU WILL SUCCEED!**

I am NOT trying to give you an EXACT script in this book to follow in your personal life. My writing is more of an outline that offers support to **YOUR** personal experiences in life. YOU need to find YOUR way through YOUR strong **SPEM HEALTHY** resolve to improve YOUR overall Health and YOUR life!

Whether the ideas in this book are completely new to you, or if they support YOUR present understanding about good mind/body/spirit health, I hope you will do YOUR best to take responsibility for the condition of YOUR overall Health. The sooner you do, the sooner you will follow this well-known, **"Serenity Prayer"** →
"God, grant me the Serenity to accept the things I cannot change, Courage to change the things I

can, and the Wisdom to know the difference." This prayer has been a big help in my life!

During **YOUR SPEM Health Journey**, make sure that you know the importance of taking time, each day, to be thankful for all the good that is in your life! Things as simple as the sight of a beautiful sunrise, or having just heard a friendly voice, or realizing how important a certain person is to you, or for your ability to touch others deeply by expressing your thoughts and feelings to them, whether it is in person, in writing, or by sign language, or for taking responsibility for your thoughts and actions while no longer feeling sorry for yourself, or for the happiness you feel in your loving relationship with God. These are just a few examples of the wonderful gifts we each have in life. No matter how big or how small, we have many positive experiences to be thankful for daily!

Often, people spend most of their time living on the defense—letting things happen, and then, reacting to their situations—rather than—living on the offense, while taking responsibility for making healthy decisions during their lifetime. This book promotes a healthy way of thinking, acting, reacting, and living!

In GOOD SPEM Health...*always!*

My SPEM Health Journey

a.) My Strong Desire to Help Others

The idea to write a book about mind/body/spirit health came to mind when my good health was abruptly taken away from me. After becoming disabled, following a serious accident, I fought hard to regain my total health! As my recovery process continued, I started to realize that my UNhealthy thoughts expressed through my UNhealthy actions caused a number of difficult experiences to come into my life. I was becoming aware that I needed to stop damaging my **Spiritual, Physical, Emotional, and Mental (SPEM) Health.**

It was by the grace of God that I made a miraculous full recovery after sustaining serious injuries in a traumatic car accident that almost took my life. This occurred when my past interests and decisions centered on drinking alcohol, getting high on pot, smoking cigarettes, and shooting pool. At (20) years of age, I was living a very irresponsible lifestyle!

After partying at a bar throughout the evening into the wee hours of the morning, and being awake for (30+) hours, I nearly **DIED** when my car, an MG Midget, found its way underneath a fully-loaded gasoline truck → **WITH ME IN IT! UNBELIEVABLE!** The rescue squad that came to the accident scene feared the gasoline truck would explode if they used electrical tools to free me from being trapped in my car underneath the trailer! Therefore, they decided to only use manual force to reach me in my car! After working (45) minutes to free me, I was rushed to a local hospital for emergency care. On top of that, the police closed that heavily traveled road for a total of two hours and fifteen minutes! A picture of this traumatic accident was on the front page of the local newspaper that day. What a way for me to become known! **OH, MY!** Glad I am still around to talk about it! Between the Ambulance, Fire, and Police personnel, I was in good hands and → **I WAS SAVED!** God bless each of those wonderful people who rescued me!

Hindsight shows me that instead of being up for so many hours partying, I should have been at home, sleeping in preparation for a new sales job I had started just six days beforehand. Instead, I was playing Russian roulette with the precious life created and given to me by my heavenly Father, God. Sadly, I was NOT paying attention to the condition of my **Spiritual, Physical, Emotional, and Mental Health,** which allowed my foolish behavior to control how I was living my life.

This book shares examples of (2) critical times in my past life when I was not following God's will. I was making **CHOICES** that were **NOT** in line with living a healthy lifestyle. Your personal concerns may have different types of experiences brought on by improper choices you have made, and will make in life! Any small and large mistakes are behavioral patterns that take us away from God's guidance as we go through life, listening only to our will, not His. As you keep your personal experiences in mind, I hope you learn to become wiser about the **CHOICES** you make in life and stop holding yourself back from improving your **SPEM Health**. Remember, God is always on YOUR side! Pray for His guidance to be shown to you as clearly as possible.

*The earth is the Lord's, and everything in it,
the world, and all who live in it;
for he founded it upon the seas and
established it upon the waters.*

~ Psalm 24

For we are God's workmanship,
created in Christ Jesus to do good works,
which God prepared in advance for us to do.

~ Ephesians 2:10

Then God said, "Let us make man
in our image, in our likeness,
and let them rule over the fish of the
sea and the birds of the air,
over the livestock, over all the earth,
and over all the creatures that
move along the ground."
So God created man in His own image,
in the image of God, he created him;
male and female he created them.

~ Genesis 1:26–27

I was unconscious when they removed me from my car and took me to a local hospital for evaluation. I had multiple lacerations, (1) puncture wound, my left lung was collapsed, my brain was swollen, and my brain stem was injured, plus, I was in a coma for (6) days and remained hospitalized for (1) month and (4) days, in (3) hospitals!

Throughout my comatose state, doctors told my family that I might die. It was a long, difficult week for them; however, miraculously, I awakened from the coma! As time moved on, I became more aware of my situation and felt an incredibly strong desire to become completely healthy again! My survival instincts helped me to work through a challenging recuperation. I am proud to be a Survivor in life!

After my complete recovery, the circumstances surrounding my accident motivated me to become interested in developing a book about improving your **SPEM Health**. I always wanted to share the important health message that YOU can become a healthy Survivor in life, too! Not just during life-threatening experiences, such as a car accident, but throughout YOUR day-to-day living!

During my lengthy recovery period and beyond, I learned to appreciate the importance of building a solid relationship with God and the value of taking better care of my **Spiritual, Physical, Emotional, and Mental Health.** God's guidance was necessary for me to gain an understanding of why I should take better care of myself during my life on earth.

Life can become so difficult for some people that they become depressed and end up not living a full life, while others give up entirely and become suicidal. Yet people like me, live, work, and have a life but make decisions that damage various aspects of their mind/body/ spirit health and contribute to bringing on more problems than they would otherwise have in life.

There are many types of misguided thoughts, inappropriate behaviors, and poor decision-making skills that can cause problems in one's life. However, many of these situations can be prevented from happening! As you start paying genuine attention to the condition of your **Spiritual, Physical, Emotional, and Mental Health**, you will begin to see where you need to make changes that will thwart UNnecessary complications from occurring in your life.

As we all know, the Bible speaks about Adam and Eve's decision to follow THEIR will, NOT God's will. When they realized the extent of their error, they suddenly felt embarrassment, shame, sadness, and other complicated emotions they had never experienced before. As they became aware of the suffering associated with THEIR decision NOT to follow God's will and ate the forbidden fruit, their lives on earth were changed forever, and so were ours!

As I lived my life on earth, I **SHOULDA** been trying to take care of my **Spiritual, Physical, Emotional, and Mental Health!** Although there will always be ups and downs in life, I **COULDA** stopped bringing added difficulties into my life by building a stronger connection with God and making healthier decisions! And if I had more respect for my body and mind, the golden temple God entrusted to me, I **WOULDA** made better choices in life! But saying **SHOULDA, COULDA, WOULDA** does nothing at all, except reinforce the fact that words alone will never change the detrimental results caused by my poor choices that brought pain and sadness into my life. **THAT'S RIGHT!** Actions speak louder than words! To find more contentment in life, I needed to dedicate my prayers, thoughts, and actions to bring healthier decisions into my mind and heart. But, instead, I was searching for contentment in all the wrong places!

How can a young man keep his way pure?
By living according to your word.

~ Psalm 119:9

Ask and it will be given to you; seek and you will find;
knock and the door will be opened to you.
For everyone who asks receives; he who seeks finds;
and to him who knocks, the door will be opened.

~ Matthew 7:7–8

The intent of this book is to encourage you to form NEW ways of looking at yourself while developing BETTER ways to take care of your mind/body/spirit health. Without a doubt, these efforts go hand-in-hand! **Achieving SPEM Health**™ points you toward focusing on **CHOICES** you have been making, which disregard the well-being of the mind/body/spirit health foundation that you were born with and can improve upon! You have the opportunity, right here and now, to either spend your time working toward improving your mind/body/spirit health condition, OR you can sit back, do nothing, and just exist in the condition you are in. **IT'S UP TO YOU!**

b.) Drawing Closer to God

Without making a concerted effort to draw closer to God, it was impossible for me to grasp His ability as the Supreme Creator of everything on earth and beyond. It may be hard to believe, but God truly understands more about each of us than we will ever be able to comprehend! He is God Almighty! He is the Master of the Universe! He knows what we are thinking and feeling before we do! He wants each of us to learn important lessons on earth, which are specifically intended for our ability to grow into the person He created us to be. And, He expects us to continually work to improve ourselves during our lives on earth.

We were each given the ability to make good quality decisions in life. We can find many answers to our questions about how to live our lives, by praying daily, reading the Bible, attending church, and having conversations and relationships with Christians AND non-Christians. Why non-Christians, also? Because we can learn and grow through all people in life. And, as we increase our Christian faith, we will start to realize when God is speaking through us to others during daily miracles, small and large. And, when God speaks to US through others, it will saturate OUR minds with deeper understandings about God's guidance.

By NOT immersing yourself in His word, how can you draw CLOSER to God and TRULY follow HIS will? You can achieve more in life while having a strong faith to build upon. By following God's will, you can learn how and why you need to make healthier choices in life.

If you do NOT attempt to learn and grow as a Christian, how can you withstand the pressures that life brings your way? How can you fully appreciate enjoyable, satisfying experiences that you have in life? Without following His Commandments (rules and guidelines), I regrettably ignored God's messages and missed opportunities for mind/body/spirit growth that I needed. **NOT GOOD!**

There are many people who say they have Christian faith, yet, do nothing to form a solid relationship with their Father, God. They do not pray on a regular basis. They rarely, if ever, go to church. And, if they attend, they leave their Christianity at the door on their way out, never deepening their connection with God. They live their lives listening and following their own thoughts and decisions, but, based on what? They do NOT search for

God's love, nor His will; therefore, their choices become extremely faulty. No matter our age or experience, we only have our limited knowledge to rely upon. But God has complete knowledge of everything that can benefit us when we are receptive to His will.

Even though human beings are born as sinners on earth, the Bible shares many examples of God's sincere loving care for us. Even though He knows we will commit sins, He understands our human desire to have free will. However, when we realize our mistakes AND stop committing sins and wrongs AND ask for His forgiveness, He amazingly wipes our slates clean, as though we never sinned at all! What a wonderful way for God to share His unconditional love with us! However, if we continue to commit the SAME sins and wrongs, we are showing Him that we have NOT learned and grown under His guidance. Therefore, we must learn how to make wise **Spiritual, Physical, Emotional, and Mental Health** CHOICES that lessen our inbred sinful nature and improve our ability to live our lives in HEALTHIER ways.

c.) Taking Responsibility for My Actions

One month **BEFORE** my traumatic car accident occurred with the gasoline tractor trailer, I had **ANOTHER** traumatic car accident! I fully believe this (1st) car accident was a strong warning, a message/lesson from God that I did NOT listen to! And because of my denial, my (2nd) car accident occurred with the gasoline tractor trailer! **HOW SAD!**

I was driving late at night. And it was dark with minimal lighting on a long, narrow, two-lane road I was on when, **SUDDENLY,** I felt a strong pain on the left side of my head as it slammed against the driver's side window of my car! In one split second, even though I was very tired and still had a buzz on after a long night of partying, I quickly realized that my car had traveled from my lane across the oncoming lane and struck something! Then without giving it a second thought, I immediately turned the steering wheel to the right to drive my car back into the lane where I had come from. **NOT SMART!** Plus, I was speeding! Hindsight shows that before I made the decision to steer my car back across the road, there was no time for me to see if the highway was clear of vehicles! I did not even think of looking! I just reacted and drove back across the road during this horribly frightening situation!

It was only by the grace of God that I made it safely back into my lane of traffic, even though my steering was now damaged. But I somehow managed to safely pull over to the side of the road and park my car. The couple of seconds that flew by felt long and terrifying! After stopping my car, I was able to figure out that I fell asleep and lost control of the steering wheel, which caused my car to veer across the road, which was usually very busy! That huge mistake could have killed me! Plus, it was such a shock to realize that my decision to abruptly drive back across the road could have ended my life! But, miraculously, BOTH times when I crossed BOTH lanes, there were NO vehicles coming toward me from EITHER direction! If there had been, the cars and the people in them would have been damaged and injured OR totaled and killed! And my car would have been totaled with me in it! My decision to drive in such an **UNhealthy SPEM** condition that night put myself AND others in grave danger!

Just the size of my car, an MG Midget, one of the smallest cars ever built, put me at an extreme disadvantage in any type of accident, let alone, also being drunk, high on marijuana, plus speeding! I honestly realized that this experience was a strong **MESSAGE from GOD** for me to straighten up and change my UNhealthy behavior!

A STRONG message/lesson sent from God…
Judy's 1st Car Accident!

My son, do not forget my teaching,
but keep my commands in your heart,
for they will prolong your life
many years and bring you prosperity.

~ Proverbs 3:1–2

Wine is a mocker and beer a brawler;
whoever is led astray by them is not wise.

~ Proverbs 20:1

If you fully obey the Lord your God
and carefully follow all his commands I give you today,
the Lord your God will set you
high above all the nations on earth.
All these blessings will come upon you
and accompany you if you obey the Lord your God.

~ Deuteronomy 28:1

He who pursues righteousness and love
finds life, prosperity and honor.

~ Proverbs 21:21

Back in those days, there were no cell phones, but fortunately, I was able to walk a short distance to a pay phone. It was very dark as I cautiously found my way to the phone. Too bad I wasn't cautious with my behavior earlier that night! I called a friend, who towed my car to a foreign car repair shop. Luckily, even at that late hour, he was able to help me. The next day, I went to a doctor and was told I had a minor concussion, plus one finger on my right hand needed to be placed in a splint due to a sprain, and my left knee was bruised. My car's front left fender was smashed, and the front left wheel was bent. Oh yes, I made up a story that I told my parents the next day, saying that a car hit mine. **BAD, JUDY!** But my story was not questioned at all. Today, I wish it would have been because parental guidance and discipline could have been helpful during my UNhealthy **SPEM CHOICES** early in life. I may NOT have been able to appreciate it then, but **I WOULD NOW!**

After my car had been repaired, I drove back to the scene of the accident hoping to figure out more details of what happened. I found a close approximation of where my car ended up and was towed from the accident scene. Plus, I retraced the tire tracks and found damage to the end of the guardrail on the opposite side of the road. And, there it was! I knew it! A message from God! After I had fallen asleep and my car drifted across the road, I was incredibly blessed to have hit the TIP of the beginning of the guardrail! YES! I say blessed because, if I had traveled across the road just a couple seconds earlier, there was no guardrail to stop my car, and I would have traveled over rocks, earth, and small bushes, and quite possibly driven over a cliff and been killed instantly! God's Message → **BE CAREFUL!**

Unless the Lord had given me help, I would
soon have dwelt in the silence of
death. When I said, "My foot is slipping,"
your love, O Lord, supported me.

~ Psalm 94:17–18

This is hard for me to admit, but even though this horrible accident got my FULL attention AND I knew that I was responsible for what happened AND I thanked God for saving my life, these realizations STILL did NOT change anything I was doing in my life! I STILL drank a lot, smoked pot, and often stayed up until the wee early morning hours, while I did NOT let the **FULL MESSAGE** from God sink in that I was living my life dangerously! **CAN YOU**

BELIEVE IT? After miraculously living through my (1ˢᵗ) traumatic car accident, I did NOT change anything at all. I continued to drink, smoke pot, stay up late at night shooting pool with my friends, while NOT having a good sense about what I was doing with my present life, nor how I was preparing for my future life. **HOW FOOLISH!**

What was I doing? Where was I going? What was my future going to be like? I had no idea of the direction that I should have been on to help myself grow into the person that God created me to be. My only interest was to bring immediate pleasurable gratification into my life. Oh, how I wish I had listened to God's important messages!

The devil helps us think that our thoughts, as UNhealthy as they are at times, are the best choices that we have. **WRONG**! We are being FOOLED to think that way because, in one way or another, when pain and despair comes into our lives, which will happen, the devil comes out the winner, not us! **HOW SAD!**

Show me your ways, O Lord, teach me your
paths; guide me in your truth and
teach me, for you are God my Savior,
and my hope is in you all day long.
Remember, O Lord, your great mercy and love,

*for they are from of old.
Remember not the sins of my youth
and my rebellious ways; according to your love
remember me, for you are good, O Lord.*

~ Psalm 25:4–7

*But you, man of God, flee from all this,
and pursue righteousness, godliness,
faith, love, endurance and gentleness.
Fight the good fight of the faith.
Take hold of eternal life to which you were
called when you made your good
confession in the presence of many witnesses.*

~ 1 Timothy 6:11–12

I do NOT blame others for my past mistakes. I know that I HAVE been and AM personally responsible for ALL decisions that I make. However, I do believe that parents could be more helpful in educating their children about planning for their present and future lives. My parents were good, honest, college grads, who loved me, and had strong Christian faith, however, I needed more discipline and guidance in my life than they were able to give to me. It is better known as, **TOUGH**

LOVE! But even when it is given, we are EACH still RESPONSIBLE for our OWN decisions!

It was too bad that I did **NOT** learn and grow after the (1st) traumatic accident I had with my car! I obviously needed to be awakened more dramatically to stop myself from traveling down the wrong road in life! And sure enough, I was given another opportunity to clearly see that I was living my life in destructive ways and received another chance to change the direction of my life. The (2nd) time, God made absolutely sure that I received His message!

We must pay more careful attention,
therefore, to what we have heard,
so that we do not drift away. For if the
message spoken by angels was binding,
and every violation and disobedience
received its just punishment,
how shall we escape if we ignore such a great salvation?
This salvation, which was first announced
by the Lord, was confirmed to us
by those who heard him. God also
testified to it by signs, wonders
and various miracles, and gifts of the

Holy Spirit distributed according to His will.

~ Hebrews 2:1–4

Teach me to do your will, for you are my God;
may your good spirit lead me on
level ground. For your name's sake,
O Lord, preserve my life;
in your righteousness, bring me out of trouble.

~ Psalm 143:10–11

One month later, as I explained earlier, I had been up for (30+) hours partying and having what I thought was a good time. I left and was on my way to work. I was drunk, high on pot, tired, and on the SAME long, narrow dangerous road I had been on when my (1ˢᵗ) car accident happened! But, this time, I was close to my work destination. Yes, with no sleep at all, I was almost safely at my job, which I had started only (6) days before-hand, and had almost gotten away with my poor choices again! **NOT GOOD!** Then, in an instant → **MY LIFE CHANGED COMPLETELY!**

Witnesses reported to the police that they saw me slapping my face in an apparent attempt to stay awake as I drove the last several tenths of a mile on this long,

25

narrow road. Before I headed into a well-known, heavily traveled, dangerous "S" curve, known as the bottleneck, I vaguely remember slapping my face, trying to stay awake, while having my radio blaring with my driver's window wide open with hopes that the loud noise and cool breeze would help me to stay awake! Clearly, those ideas did NOT work because sure enough, I fell asleep while driving again, just like I did in my (1ˢᵗ) car accident one month prior to this date! Hindsight being 20/20 shows that if I would have learned a valuable lesson from my (1ˢᵗ) car accident, my (2ⁿᵈ) car accident → **COULD HAVE BEEN PREVENTED!** Oh, how I wish I would have learned!

As I entered the sharp "S" curve, my tiny MG Midget drifted over the double lines into the oncoming lane, then came back into the correct lane that I was traveling in, before drifting into the wrong lane of traffic → **AGAIN!** Since I had driven my car back into the correct lane, I must have been awake long enough to realize the change of my car's direction, but I was obviously only able to correct it the first time my car drifted across the double lines → **NOT THE SECOND TIME!**

As my car drifted across the road into the opposing lane of traffic for the second time, I was traveling directly toward the left, middle-side of a gasoline tractor trailer fully loaded with 8,000 gallons of fuel! I was told about my accident, but, I had no memory of what happened. Later, I saw a picture of my car underneath the trailer on the front page of the local newspaper, which allowed me to see the result of my accident → **FOR THE FIRST TIME!** It was dreadful looking! The story also appeared in other newspapers throughout Pennsylvania. It was a VERY traumatic AND horrifying car accident!

As hard as it is to believe, my car and I ended up directly underneath the trailer of the fully loaded gasoline truck! The impact of my car hitting the truck's rear axles only bent it a bit. But my beloved car was totaled, and I was critically injured → **INSIDE OF IT!** Though I was fortunate to have been in a car so low to the ground, because, if it had been any higher in size, I could have been decapitated as I traveled underneath the tractor trailer! **NOT GOOD!**

'Bottleneck' crash

This accident at 8:15 a.m. today in the "bottleneck" at ███████ sent a woman to ███████ Hospital where she was then transferred to ███████ Hospital. She was listed in critical condition. Her name was not released pending notification of the next of kin. The "bottleneck" was closed until 10:30.

After NOT learning a month earlier from
a message/lesson sent from God…
Judy's 2nd Car Accident!

The truck driver did not know that he had a car underneath his trailer, so he kept driving through the "S" curve, dragging my car underneath his truck farther down the road! He finally came to a halt after noticing people in other cars motioning to him that something was wrong! His tractor trailer stopped just before he approached the end of the "S" curve. At the light, he ended up stopping close to the area where my car had entered the "S" curve just a few seconds beforehand.

Numerous people, who witnessed this disturbing accident, called the police to report it. Fortunately, this was a well-known, well-traveled area, so the Ambulance, Fire, and Police personnel were able to arrive within a few short minutes. However, seeing me in my car, trapped underneath the tractor trailer, must have been a horrific site to witness, and frightening, too! If it had exploded, businesses nearby would have been destroyed and many people would have been injured, and/or, killed, including me! Even the emergency personnel were shocked and amazed to see my little car completely parallel underneath this fully loaded gasoline tractor trailer! In the blink of an eye, or I should say, with my closed eyes, this accident changed my present and future life dramatically!

This is what the Lord says—your Redeemer,
the Holy One of Israel: "I am the Lord your God,
who teaches you what is best for you,
who directs you in the way you should go.
If only you had paid attention to my commands,
your peace would have been like a river,
your righteousness like the waves of the sea."

~ Isaiah 48:17–18

While the emergency personnel worked to remove me from my car and I was moved to a hospital nearby, the bottleneck was closed for a total of two hours and fifteen minutes! **OH, MY!** I found out, later in time, that when they finally got to me in my car, I was slumped over in the driver's seat, not moving at all. After they removed me and checked my vital signs, they found that I was in a comatose state. Although I was responsible for this accident, God was watching over me. He does NOT always stop things from happening in our lives, but He does help us learn and grow from our experiences. This was **MY TIME** to **LEARN** to **STOP** ignoring God's important messages!

Create in me a pure heart, O God,
and renew a steadfast spirit within me.
Do not cast me from your presence
or take your Holy Spirit from me.
Restore to me the joy of your salvation
and grant me a willing spirit, to sustain me.

~ Psalm 51:10–12

Consider it pure joy, my brothers,
whenever you face trials of many kinds,
because you know that the testing of
your faith develops perseverance.
Perseverance must finish its work so that
you may be mature and complete, not lacking anything.

~ James 1:2–4

d.) Choices in Life

Prior to experiencing both of my traumatic car accidents, I had been ignoring each aspect of my **Spiritual, Physical, Emotional, and Mental Health.** As a result, I suffered the ultimate consequence of nearly causing my own death! It was only when I took responsibility for the improper choices I had been making that I began my journey to find and retain better overall **SPEM Health.** When I became fully open to seeing and admitting to my imperfections, I was able to see myself and the world around me more clearly. It was then that I started to make constructive changes in my behavior and, eventually, could feel my life becoming more peaceful. It was an upward climb with lots of ups-and-downs, let me tell you!

How long the process takes is NOT written in stone! Everyone is on their **OWN** timetable; however, certain steps must take place early on that will aid in bringing healthy changes into your life. Starting with the understanding that YOU are in control of the choices YOU make in relation to YOUR actions and reactions! God will guide YOU, but it is in YOUR hands to improve YOUR actual decisions on earth. **DO NOT FORGET**, God expects each of us to care for the precious body and life He has given us!

Don't you know that you yourselves
are God's temple and that
God's Spirit lives in you? If anyone destroys
God's temple, God will destroy him;
for God's temple is sacred, and you are that temple.

~ 1 Corinthians 3:16–17

Was it simple for me to take responsibility for MY choices? **Absolutely NOT!** Will it be easy for you to do? **Probably NOT!** But the hardest part is getting started! Sadly, as I stated, I waited until I almost lost my life before admitting that I had a problem and needed to make healthy changes. I became committed to my goal of learning why I was making decisions that caused problems to occur in my life. And as my wisdom grew, I became able to institute **NEW** habits that would help me take better care of myself. Did I experience **BACK-SLIDES?** Yes, I did, but as time went on, I continued to adjust my thoughts, feelings, and actions much better.

As I worked hard to decipher my past and present thoughts and behavior, I often struggled to find the **Emotional and Mental** strength to fully comprehend what I was uncovering. I prayed to God daily for the ability to get rid of damaging habits that contributed to the UNhealthiness in my life and replace them with better, healthier ones. Fortunately, I had honestly grown tired of making decisions that brought problems to me! Including getting myself **NOWHERE** in life!

During my journey to get to know myself, I felt like I was on a nonstop roller-coaster ride with a mixture of ups and downs surrounding my effort to closely examine the ingredients of my **Emotional and Mental Health** makeup. My feelings and thoughts, needing to be healed, were primarily based on painful experiences that were self-inflicted or introduced to me by others. Fortunately, I was willing to work through the pain involved to gain greater knowledge about my inner self. Many of **MY CHOICES** in life had been incredibly hurtful to me and disrespectful to God! I did not want to live like that any longer!

Thanks to sticking with my important goals of becoming closer to God's will and learning to treat myself better, I find it a joy to give testimonials today that thanks to working at it hard enough, my life has become better! I hope my experience will be an example that shows you can surmount the difficulties in your life, as well.

My soul is weary with sorrow;
strengthen me according to your word.
Keep me from deceitful ways;
be gracious to me through your law.
I have chosen the way of truth;
I have set my heart on your laws.

~ Psalm 119:28–30

Teach me, O Lord, to follow your decrees;
then I will keep them to the end.
Give me understanding, and I will keep your
law and obey it with all my heart.
Direct me in the path of your commands,
for there I find delight.
Turn my heart toward your statutes
and not toward selfish gain.
Turn my eyes away from worthless things;
preserve my life according to
your word. Fulfill your promise to your
servant, so that you may be feared.
Take away the disgrace I dread, for your laws are good.
How I long for your precepts!
Preserve my life in your righteousness.

~ Psalm 119:33–40

Even though my life continues to have difficult times, they are within the normal ebb and flow of discomforts in life and much more manageable now! I am no longer saddled with preventable problems coming into my life caused by my UNhealthy **Emotional and Mental** rebellion that contributed to my UNwise choices in the past. I finally came to realize that, one way or another, I am responsible for **ALL THE CHOICES** that I make in life, including how I react to everything that happens to me! YES, even as a VICTIM of circumstances, it is up to me to react PROPERLY. No one can force me to act improperly, except myself!

> *As obedient children, do not conform*
> *to the evil desires you had*
> *when you lived in ignorance.*
>
> ~ Peter 1:14

> *"The good man brings good things out of the*
> *good stored up in him, and the evil*
> *man brings evil things out of the evil stored*
> *up in him. But I tell you that*
> *men will have to give account on the day*
> *of judgment for every careless word they have spoken.*

37

For by your words you will be acquitted,
and by your words you will be condemned."

~ Matthew 12:35–37

Time-and-time again, I have pondered why many people do not attempt to change THEIR irrational way of living, while, at the same time, placing culpability on others (even God!) for situations they say are beyond THEIR control! Oh, how sad! THEY blame others for being responsible for THEIR lot in life! **THEIR UNhealthy behavior** goes on for years as they continue to have serious difficult times due to THEIR choices in life!

Did you notice that I said, **"THEIR CHOICES** in life"? When we blame anyone other than ourselves for OUR problems in life, we will NEVER grow from where we are. Consequently, we become stunted in becoming all of whom God created us to be and our life continues to have unsettling troubles strewn throughout it!

If you think about it, generally speaking **MANY PEOPLE ARE LAZY!** It seems easier for many to just sit back and let the world go "round-and-round" than to get motivated to make critical changes in **THEIR "little**

corners of the world." I realized that **MY CHOICE** to deepen my faith in God, while working diligently to understand my mind/body/spirit connections enabled me to improve how I was managing my life. I knew this pleased God! He is extremely interested in helping us reach a healthier state of being on earth!

And without faith it is impossible to please God,
because anyone who comes to him must believe
that he exists and that he rewards
those who earnestly seek him.

~ Hebrews 11:6

And we know that in all things God works
for the good of those who love him,
who have been called according to his purpose.

~ Romans 8:28

We have different gifts according to the
grace given us. If a man's gift is
prophesizing, let him use it in proportion to
his faith. If it is serving, let him serve.
If it is teaching, let him teach. If it is
encouraging, let him encourage.

If it is contributing to the needs of others,
let him give generously. If it is leadership,
let him govern diligently. If it is showing mercy,
let him do it cheerfully.

~ Romans 12:6–8

People need to realize that **THEIR** thoughts, feelings, actions, and reactions are primarily based on how **THEY** feel about **THEMSELVES!** Feeling negatively about yourself is a key reason you will make damaging decisions. This, in turn, causes tribulations to occur as you deal with your life experiences! When you take responsibility to rid yourself of debilitating thoughts and behavioral patterns, you will find a new comfort level for yourself in God's eyes, other's eyes, and → **IN YOUR VERY OWN EYES!**

Even though I walk through the valley of the
shadow of death, I will fear no evil,
for you are with me; your rod and
your staff, they comfort me.

~ Psalm 23:4

e.) My Three Hospital Stays

I had been traveling through life with no direction, and although I believed in God, I was UNcaring of God's plan for my life. However, after my (2nd) traumatic car accident, I was forced to no longer see myself as a "party girl." I was now a broken person, no longer a physically healthy individual. I had the title of being disabled. **WHOA! Wait a minute → ME?** Come on! It can't be true! I was only (20) years old and healthy! I was having fun! How could I have been knocked out of the game of life like that? But I was UNable to live independently while needing others to take care of me daily. I did not like my situation at all, nor that it had taken two traumatic experiences to help me finally see my mistakes in life more clearly!

And the God of all grace, who called
you to his eternal glory in Christ,
after you have suffered a little while,
will himself restore you and make you
strong, firm and steadfast. To him be the
power for ever and ever. Amen.

~ 1 Peter 5:10–11

Now this is what the Lord Almighty says:
"Give careful thought to your ways.

~ Haggai 1:5

Do not be wise in your own eyes;
fear the Lord and shun evil.
This will bring health to your body
and nourishment to your bones.

~ Proverbs 3:7–8

Thankfully, my skull was not fractured, but my brain was swollen, and the (6) day coma was due to hitting my head and my brain stem being injured. Did you know that the brain stem controls ALL voluntary and involuntary functions in the body? I sure made a mess of things for myself, didn't I?

From the accident site, I had been taken to a nearby hospital in a comatose state, initially thrashing around on the gurney as they brought me into the emergency room. I was later told that it took several men to hold me down! However, I was totally UNable to communicate and moved uncontrollably. So they tied me down, conducted vital assessments, sutured my various lacerations and puncture wound, and treated my collapsed lung. Then they transferred me to a (2ⁿᵈ) Hospital nearby, which had the necessary equipment to study and treat my life-threatening brain injuries.

Earlier that same year, my father accepted a job in Western, Pennsylvania, and my parents planned to move there. I told them I wanted to stay in Central, Pennsylvania, to start my independent life and would not be going with them. My parents tried to change my mind, but I would not budge on my decision. I was ready to strike out on my own.

After both of my parents arrived at the Hospital, one of the emergency room doctors involved with my care truthfully said, "If your daughter does not die, she might be completely disabled for life."

My mother asked the doctor if there was any chance that I would NOT die and that I COULD return to being completely healthy again. The doctor agreed that it was possible, but he declared that it was a long shot! My parents prayed for me to live and to make a complete recovery.

*And the prayer offered in faith will
make the sick person well;
the Lord will raise him up.
If he has sinned, he will be forgiven.*

~ James 5:15

*Jesus looked at them and said,
"With man this is impossible,
but with God all things are possible."*

~ Matthew 19:26

*Turn, O Lord, and deliver me;
save me because of your unfailing love.*

~ Psalm 6:4

Although I have no memory of my week in ICU, nor much of my time as a patient in (3) Hospitals, I was told that my family and friends were with me daily in the ICU, though only two people at a time and short visits were allowed. I am so sorry that **MY POOR CHOICES** in life caused such a tremendous amount of pain for everyone who cared about me. Believe me, I am so sorry for causing everyone so much concern about my well-being. **I TRULY AM!**

The medical personnel were uncertain if my voluntary and involuntary nervous systems were functioning properly. They inserted a breathing apparatus into my airway and continually monitored my vital signs for heart rate, blood pressure, respiration rate, and body temperature, while oxygen was flowing through a nasal cannula, a small tube under my nose, and a wide tube was sticking out of the left side of my chest to remove excess fluid accumulating in my collapsed lung. I was holding my left arm and leg in a fetal position, which is a common occurrence with brain injury patients. Before this accident, I was a physically healthy, lively, athletic gal with an outgoing personality. I can just imagine how difficult it must have been for my family and friends to see me in such an immobilized state!

I responded to pain stimulation but did not communicate in any other way. Then, during my sixth day in ICU, while I continued to be in a comatose state, a friend of mine was at my bedside, visiting me. He and I regularly played pool together at another bar I used to frequent. At that time, we were alone. He was telling me that he had a gift for me, a book about shooting pool.

I slowly opened my eyes, looked at him, and mumbled past the tube in my mouth, "What the f * * * happened?"

He was pleased to see that I had awakened and was also trying to talk! Albeit, not in a very polite manner! It was nothing short of a **MIRACLE**! He quickly told a nurse that I came out of the coma and had spoken! My family was thrilled to get the miraculous news that I was awake! They were equally thrilled to hear that my being in a critical condition and possibly dying was becoming a remote possibility, **THANK GOD!**

When the hospital staff realized that I was stable and out of critical condition, they moved me into a semi-private room on a Med Surg floor. After I was moved into the new room, I essentially needed to learn how to do things again. Walking, talking, and thinking had become actions that were "fuzzy" to me. It was wonderful that my body was on the mend, but my brain needed to be "retrained" to regain control of my voluntary bodily functions. Praise God that all of my involuntary functions worked well throughout my stay in this hospital for (25) days.

While in the semiprivate room, I was allowed to have more visitors. I was told that my parents and friends came to be with me. As I mentioned earlier, I only had a minimal amount of memory while I was in all three hospitals. I really do not recall more than a few fragmented scenes and conversations, at best. But, I appreciate their love and thoughtfulness for coming to see me!

I recall being upset that my beautiful car was totaled and sitting in a junkyard! My car was very important to me! I was glad that a good friend of mine went to the junkyard and took pictures of my car, which I still have today. What a sight! Plus, I had just put four brand-new Pirelli tires on my little sports car, which cost $100 each! I know they could have been taken off and sold, but my parents were obviously not interested in doing anything other than sitting by my side and praying for my full recovery. I understand! I appreciate everyone who came to be with me AND all the prayers being said for my complete healing to occur.

Here's an odd story! Less than a year before my (2nd) car accident with the gasoline tractor trailer, I used to joke around with my friends about my car being small enough to fit underneath the side of a tractor trailer! **HONEST!** Several times, I had driven my little MG Midget up to the side of a parked tractor trailer to prove that it could just fit underneath the trailer portion! And, get this! I, also, remember telling myself that if I ever died, I wanted to die in that car. That's how much I loved it! My thinking in life was really messed up, wasn't it? Be careful what you pray for in YOUR life!

I was surprised, (3) years after my accident, when a man walked up to me at my employment and said, "I know who you are! We worked together a few years ago. I have (2) pictures I'd like to give to you."

He left and came back later that week to give me two **UNBELIEVABLE PHOTOS!** In the PHOTO on Page 50, if you look closely, you will see a Fire Truck driving around a curve toward the scene of my accident. That means the rescue personnel were just arriving and I was **TRAPPED,** unconscious in my sports scar at that → **EXACT TIME!** And, in the PHOTO on Page 51, if you look closely, you will see a white fire hose stretched across the road! I had already been **REMOVED** from my sports car.

God surely wanted to make sure that I received His message loud and clear through the man who delivered those pictures to me! **YES, GOD! MESSAGE RECEIVED! LESSON BEING LEARNED!**

In this **PHOTO,** if you look closely, you
will see a Fire Truck driving around a curve
toward the scene of my 2nd accident!

In this **PHOTO,** if you look closely,
you will see a white fire hose stretched
across the road in my 2nd accident!

While I was in the hospital, the nurses fed me breakfast, lunch, and dinner in my semiprivate room. They, also, pounded on my back to help get the fluid out of my collapsed lung while the drainage tube continued to assist with that process.

One day, a nurse walked into my room to feed me and caught me eating on my own! My food tray had been brought into my room, and apparently, I did not want to wait for a nurse to come in and help me eat it. I wanted it right then! I must have been feeding myself fairly well, because, after that incident, I was told the nurses never fed me again! ha! ha! I have always been a very determined individual! ha! ha!

I had another few interesting episodes in the semi-private room. There were several times, after the drainage tube was removed from the side of my chest, when I was found in my roommate's bed! YEP! I was obviously still living on the edge! ha! ha! When I was alone, I would somehow get out of my bed, stumble over to the other bed in the room, climb in, and go to sleep! Why I did that, I have no idea! Fortunately, the other patient was NEVER in her bed when I climbed in! That would have been a very → **BAD CHOICE!**

It was extremely dangerous for me to attempt to stand and walk because my body was still on the mend. I had been immobile for a long time. Plus, I had an injury to my left knee, and my brain and body were only moderately back in sync. I was NOT able to support my FULL body weight yet! So, to stop me from being able to move around in the room, the doctors and nurses decided to restrain me with a chest strap to prevent me from getting out of my bed again.

Yet one day, I clearly wanted to get out of bed and go to the bathroom on my own! I actually have a vague memory of working extremely hard to squirm out of the restraint that was strapped tightly over my chest and tied to the lower sides of my bed. Eventually, somehow, I got myself out of it without untying it from the bed! It must have loosened up; otherwise, it was a move that only Houdini could have made! After getting out of the restraint, I stumbled to the bathroom and promptly fell down and hit my head on the bathroom floor! My bits of memory included getting out of bed and suddenly feeling terrible pain in my head while having some knowledge that I was on the floor. A nurse eventually found me and got me back into bed. My family, doctors, and nurses were all fearful that my brain was injured again!

But, after testing was finished, I received a huge blessing from God! I did NOT suffer any problems whatsoever from that fall!

At that time, there was another young woman in the hospital around my age, who was a patient, with a brain stem injury, also. She suffered her injury from a car accident as well. Our mothers supported each other quite a bit. However, that patient had brain seizures, took medication for the seizures, had fluid buildup on the brain, and she needed to have brain surgery. Her brain injury certainly resulted in a much worse medical situation than mine.

I thought about her for years and prayed that she made a full recovery. Her situation showed me that one person's experience, no matter how similar to another person's experience, can end up with totally different results. God has reasons for everything that He allows to happen to each of us AND to those around us.

"For I know the plans I have for you," declares the Lord,
"plans to prosper you and not to harm you,
plans to give you hope and a future."
~ Jeremiah 29:11

ACHIEVING SPEM HEALTH
SPIRITUAL PHYSICAL EMOTIONAL MENTAL
(IT'S UP TO YOU!)™

[The Lord who] redeems your life from the pit

and crowns you with love and compassion,

who satisfies your desires with good things

so that your youth is renewed like the eagle's.

~ Psalm 103:4–5

f.) My Unhappy Forced Move

I had timed it just right! Less than one month BEFORE my (2nd) car accident, I had secured a sales job and a small, one-bedroom apartment to move into just a couple days before my parents and oldest brother were moving into their new home across the state. My other older brother already moved out of our home a few years earlier to attend college in another state. Our family had moved three times in the past. The first move occurred when I was only (3) years of age, which did not affect me. The moves that occurred when I was (11) and (14) years of age were difficult for me to experience. I was not happy about uprooting myself again and moving at (20) years old. Even though we lived in Central Pennsylvania for only six years, my roots had grown there, and I did not want to move again.

The date of my family's move was exactly (3) weeks AFTER the date of my accident with the gasoline tractor trailer. I can only imagine what a difficult time that was for them. Moving itself is a big deal! PLUS, there I was in a hospital, **Spiritually** UNhinged, **Physically** DISabled, **Emotionally** and **Mentally** UNaware of what was going on, and totally UNable to take care of myself independently! My parents made the only logical, loving choice they could and had me transferred to a hospital just a few miles away from their new home. These must have been stressful days for my family! I am glad they had each other and God to lean on for support!

Just six days before my (2nd) car accident, I had started working as a commissioned salesperson. Today, I do not see how I would have been able to withstand the financial pressures of living on my own as I had planned with no solid form of income. Either way, whether I would have handled it or not, my dream of living on my own in Central Pennsylvania had vanished due to → **MY FOOLISH CHOICES!** It seemed like several big difficulties were coming into my life ALL because I did **NOT** listen to God's **FIRST** warning, His message/lesson for me to make **Healthy SPEM** changes to improve the direction of my life!

> *"For my thoughts are not your thoughts,*
> *neither are your ways my ways,"*
> *declares the Lord. "As the heavens are*
> *higher than the earth, so are*
> *my ways higher than your ways and my*
> *thoughts than your thoughts."*
>
> ~ Isaiah 55:8–9

I have a vague remembrance of being transferred by ambulance to the (3rd) Hospital where I would be a patient. I was happy that my mother lovingly sat next to me in the ambulance for the long trip. The driver was kind and considerate of my ill health and limitations, so we only made one stop for something to eat along the way. Otherwise, we traveled straight through while I slept during most of the trip. I had been sleeping a lot every day and night in the hospital, so that was not unusual.

I was a patient in the (3rd) Hospital for (9) additional days before being released to start my life in my family's new home (34) days after my accident. My brain was not quite functioning properly yet, and it took several months before I became more like my old self again. I do remember an unusual situation. My mother was with me in my hospital room, a private one this time, and I was talking more and more, unlike in the past days. I recall her asking me, "Judy, why are you talking like you are from the South?"

I suddenly heard myself speaking with a Southern accent in my voice! After her question, I totally stopped speaking that way! It is a mystery to me why it happened. But, I think there might have been a hospital employee with a Southern accent, which I heard while being in a coma. Perhaps that sound entered my mind, and my brain took it on as my own? I do not know, but let's remember, there is no absolute knowledge about whether people can hear anything while being in a coma; however, it is an interesting possibility!

Fortunately, I had peaceful days and nights for the remainder of my final hospital stay, as my brain and body were on the mend. Later though, after I was fully discharged from the (3rd) Hospital, a strong sense of survivor's guilt came over my mind and heart. That feeling stayed with me for many years as I realized that I was in a minority of people who successfully AND completely survived traumatic brain injuries. I kept wondering why I was saved so miraculously, while some others are not.

Compared to the young woman in the (2nd) Hospital, who suffered from her brain injuries to a larger degree than I did, it showed my family, and later myself, that even though my brain injuries were severe, three more miracles came into my life! I was blessed to never need brain surgery! I never had seizures! And when I was released from the (3rd) Hospital, I did not need to be on any medicine whatsoever! I was truly blessed!

After leaving the hospital, my family doctor kept me under his care for close to a year as my brain and body healed completely. The medical tests I took throughout that year showed that I had fully recovered from my injuries. All of my motor skills, memory, intellect, senses, and physical abilities were fully intact. The only residual was my left knee's ACL (Anterior Cruciate Ligament) was slightly torn, apparently from being slammed against the dashboard in my car. My two-seater sports car did not have seatbelts built in it. They were not mandatory as they are now.

Although it is difficult to understand why I survived with fewer complications than other people did, I continue to trust that God knows what He is doing. I have come to believe that everything in life is connected in one way or another. When something happens to one of us, it affects other people in various ways. Apparently, one person's situation has different results than other people's situations, so all those touched by each person's experience can **learn AND grow** in ways that are specific to their needs in life.

I prayed daily (and still do) for everyone to receive answers to their prayers while accepting God's will if the answer is NOT what they were seeking. I have been extremely grateful to God for saving me AND putting me on the road to improve my life by helping me learn to take better care of my mind/body/spirit foundation.

My way of dealing with myself, back then, was neither heavenly NOR healthy! I did NOT care about myself in healthy Christian ways. I was ignoring my **SPEM Health** that I should have been nurturing in much better ways! I am forever grateful that God gave me another chance to correct my mistakes and live a fuller life on earth. He can do that for you, too! Stay open to His **MESSAGES!**

Good and upright is the Lord; therefore
he instructs sinners in his ways.
He guides the humble in what is right
and teaches them his way.
~ Psalm 25: 8–9

My doctor did not allow me to drive for (6) months, yet I was eager to become whole again and do everything I had been able to do before my accident, without any limitations at all. Thankfully, I had NO phobia about driving again, which was probably because I had NO memory of the accident. I would like to think of it as a gift from God, but having amnesia about my accident was medically caused due to my brain injuries. Otherwise, the memory of driving my car underneath a fully-loaded gasoline truck might have caused a deep-seated FEAR to occur for me!

But what a situation! I was not where I wanted to live. This was an UNhappy forced move for me. I was ready to start my independent life. So can you imagine how I felt? Here I was still getting my "senses" together as my injuries were healing, yet I felt so out-of-place with where I was in life! **MY POOR** decision-making skills really put me in a difficult situation, and I was certainly suffering the consequences of my actions! I must repeat that if I had made **BETTER** decisions, these partic-ular problems would **NOT** have occurred in my life. Instead, I would have been learning how to get through life on my own while facing an entirely different set of problems.

What decisions have **YOU** made that are present-ing difficult times in **YOUR** life? Ponder that question as deeply as you can! That is one of the first steps you need to take in your quest of, **Achieving SPEM Health** and developing a better life. Another step you should take is either to make new decisions on your own, which can be done, and/or, find a competent therapist to guide you to uncover Healthy ways to **ADJUST** your thinking AND decision-making skills. Plus, ask God to help guide you during this process. He loves **YOU** and will **NEVER** leave your side!

> *If we deliberately keep on sinning after we*
> *have received the knowledge of the truth,*
> *no sacrifice for sins is left, but only a fearful*
> *expectation of judgment and of*
> *raging fire that will consume the enemies of God.*
> ~ Hebrews 10:26–27

> *I will give you a new heart and put a new*
> *spirit in you; I will remove from you*
> *your heart of stone and give you a heart of*
> *flesh. And I will put my Spirit in you*
> *and move you to follow my decrees*
> *and be careful to keep my laws.*
> ~ Ezekiel 36:26–27

Nine months later, even though I was still considered medically disabled, I moved back to Central

Pennsylvania to start my independent life. Before I left, my family doctor said, "You'll be back."

I smiled and said, "I don't think so!"

My voluntary and involuntary bodily functions were back to normal, but my doctor said my brain was still sensitive and healing throughout. So he decided to keep me on the disabled list a bit longer.

My mother was troubled that I was making plans to move. The fact that I was leaving and still disabled was certainly part of her reasoning. Plus, my parents were nearing (60) years of age and knew the stumbling blocks in life would now be more difficult for what I was facing, being disabled with no family nearby, and no job. At least I had applied for and was receiving monthly disability payments, thanks to my having been employed when my accident occurred. Plus, I was, also, looking for a new job.

I had become sad about living in a new area where I did not know anyone except my family. I was no longer in school, I was not working, and I was disabled. I just could not see myself staying there. And my biggest reasoning was that I had already made the "emotional" break to leave home, but that dream vanished because of my accident.

I basically stayed in my (9 x 9) bedroom day and night, only coming out for meals. Otherwise, I stayed there all cooped up, only thinking about how I could get out of there. I phoned friends of mine and was in contact a lot with a good friend who lived in a state out West. She really helped me keep my sanity! We spoke often by phone and wrote to each other frequently. She was a true life saver!

My parents and brother were good-hearted people, but, I found it unbearable to stay with them any longer. It was my time to move on, or should I say → **GO AND GROW!** So, after finding an open apartment, that a friend told me about, I moved back to Central Pennsylvania (9) months after my accident! Yes, my new journey was filled with a lot of ups and downs, let me tell you! Hindsight shows me that I had stepped into a challenging lifestyle! But, I was eager to be on my own! I was afraid to drink alcohol and smoke pot, especially since my brain was still healing. So, I stayed off both for a couple years, then started again, though nothing like in the past. However, this was **MY BACKSLIDE!** It took a bit longer, but I soon stopped smoking pot completely and, later, only drank occasionally. However, I was still smoking cigarettes. **VERY FOOLISH!**

God is a loving God who helps us live better lives on earth in preparation for eternal life in heaven. Without God's guidance, I do not know how I could have successfully survived all the difficulties that were a part of my life.

g.) Life After My Hospitalization

Through the years, God's Spirit flourished within me as I grew to understand how much He loved me and wanted me to take better care of myself. Too bad it could not happen overnight, but over time, I realized that I needed to build better **SPEM Health** habits to improve my life. I was and am forever thankful to have been miraculously blessed with a chance to live my life in a better, healthier way. It was up to me to learn to cherish His temple within the earthly body that He has given to me and to always treat my mind and body with respect and care. Taking care of my **SPEM Health was finally becoming important to me!**

Do you not know that your body is the temple of the Holy Spirit who is in you, whom you have received from God? You are not your own; you were bought at a price; Therefore, honor God in your body.

I finally understood that filling my body with alcohol, drugs, poor thoughts, and ungodly decisions were sins and wrongs that I committed while being among others who were mistreating themselves in similar ways. It was **NOT** a **SPEM Healthy** way to live my life. It was **NOT the road** that God wanted me to be on!

My prayers continue daily for everyone to realize how they are mistreating themselves. Whether you purchased this book for yourself, a loved one, or a friend, I pray that you each learn how to save yourself from unnecessary difficulties coming into your life. I encourage you to do the work involved to improve the way you are living your life. Stop **UNproductive SPEM HABITS** that are ingrained into your daily routines and replace them with **Productive SPEM HABITS** that will enable you to develop a better lifestyle! I am proof that this can be done! Build a strong connection with God so you can develop a deeper knowledge of getting through life on earth in healthier ways. Your effort will guide you to travel on the road that He knows is best for you in life.

To support your growing **Spiritual Health,** try talking with other Christians, get involved with church support groups, read the Bible, and pray daily to God.

It would also be wise to set up an appointment with your family doctor, and if you do not have one, find one nearby. Ask for a complete physical each year. This will include a blood test, which will show you if there are any problems lurking within your body. Your PCP— Primary Care Provider (MD, DO, PA, NP) will guide you on how to improve medical problems you might have and provide ongoing care for more serious problems. Remember! If you have NO problems at all, that will be encouraging to learn as well. Going in for your annual **Physical Health** assessment will give you an important understanding of your health from head-to-toe.

You should also take care of your **Emotional and Mental Health** by seeking counseling from professional therapists (social workers/counselors, psychologists, psychiatrists) as needed. Your PCP should be able to recommend good, qualified therapists to assist you with counseling, and/or, medicines that may be needed.

Hey! Nothing in life comes easily, so do not fear the art of learning how to stay ahead of **Spiritual, Physical, Emotional, and Mental Health** problems that can come about. Make **Healthy SPEM** decisions TODAY to help protect against problems TOMORROW!

Always be aware of ways the devil will tempt you and try to suck the good godly life right out of you! There are many temptations in life; however, YOU can decide NOT to let them become a part of your present life. Remember, YOU have the power to say, "Yes" or "No." YOU have the choice to accept OR reject thoughts and ideas that have negative consequences for

YOUR present and future life on earth. Please do NOT do what I did and ignore the wrong roads you may be traveling on. Make the adjustments you need in your life, **TODAY!**

Be responsible and choose to live the life that God has planned for YOU. As you grow in His word, messages/lessons will come your way, which will make you a stronger Christian. **HALLELUJAH!**

Be self-controlled and alert. Your enemy the devil
prowls around like a roaring
lion looking for someone to devour.
Resist him, standing firm in the faith, because
you know that your brothers throughout the world
are undergoing the same kind of sufferings.
~ 1 Peter 5:8–9

In the same way, count yourselves dead to sin
but alive to God in Christ Jesus.
Therefore do not let sin reign in your
mortal body so that you obey its evil desires.
Do not offer the parts of your body
to sin, as instruments of wickedness,
but rather offer yourselves to God,

as those who have been brought
from death to life; and offer
the parts of your body to him
as instruments of righteousness.
For sin shall not be your master,
because you are not under law, but under grace.

~ Romans 6:11–14

Therefore, since Christ suffered in his body,
arm yourselves also with the same attitude,
because he who has suffered in his body
is done with sin. As a result, he does not
live the rest of his earthly life for
evil human desires, but rather for the will of God.
For you have spent enough time
in the past doing what pagans choose to do—
living in debauchery, lust, drunkenness,
orgies, carousing and detestable idolatry.
They think it strange that you do not
plunge with them into the same flood
of dissipation, and they heap abuse on you.
But they will have to give account to him
who is ready to judge the living and the dead.

~ 1 Peter 4:1–5

*When tempted, no one should say, "God is
tempting me." For God cannot be
tempted by evil, nor does he tempt anyone;
but each one is tempted when, by his own
evil desire, he is dragged away and enticed.
Then, after desire has conceived, it gives birth to sin;
and sin, when it is full-grown, gives birth to death.*

~ James 1:13–15

*Do not conform any longer to the pattern of this world,
but be transformed by the renewing of your mind.
Then you will be able to test and approve
what God's will is—his good, pleasing and perfect will.*

~ Romans 12:2

*Be very careful, then, how you live—
not as unwise but as wise,
making the most of every opportunity,
because the days are evil.
Therefore do not be foolish, but understand
what the Lord's will is.*

~ Ephesians 5:15–17

I came to realize that my poor behavior was only growing worse day by day. Too bad **I ALMOST KILLED MYSELF** before I realized that I needed to change my thoughts and actions! Thankfully, God never gave up on me, nor will He ever give up on you! If you feel yourself crying out to Him for mercy, realize that He is ready and willing to forgive you for your sins and wrongs. He just wants to hear that you are sincerely asking for His forgiveness and want to repent. Tell Him that you believe His son, Jesus Christ, died on the cross so your sins could be forgiven and forgotten forever.

At times, we will each struggle in our efforts to understand what we need to learn. Remember, whether we find immediate answers or not, we need to **STAY OPEN** to receive and understand God's will so we can live our lives to the fullest potential.

Keep in mind that everything happens in God's time. Although we may be eager for a situation to work out this way, that way, or our way, we must wait on God's way in His time! Once you become skilled at being open and receptive to hearing God's direction for your life, you need to also be patient to receive it. In other words, God knows when **YOU** will be **READY** to move on to **YOUR NEW LESSONS**.

After I developed a **DEEPER** connection with God, I canNOT count the number of times when answers to my prayers came to my awareness when I least expected it. Why? Because the answers came when He **KNEW** I was **READY** to receive them! He knows which **LESSONS** we need to **LEARN** before we move from where we are in our Christian growth process.

As you pray, open your mind, heart, and soul, as I finally did to start making better decisions! Remember, you are the only one holding yourself back! Ask God to help you get out of the destructive, UNhealthy ruts you are living in. Choose to follow His will, and He will guide you to understand how you can improve the choices you make every day of your life on earth. He is a wonderful, caring Father, who waits for us to **Honor AND Cherish Him!**

Now here is a curveball to consider! Our decisions, no matter how perfect they seem to us, no matter how much we pray for proper decisions to come to us, no matter how much we believe in the decisions we make, the results will **NOT** always be what we had hoped for! God does **NOT** eliminate all difficult situations from occurring in our life, though He does help us work through experiences we become involved in. God real-

izes that there are times when we must go through difficulties to be able to learn and grow more effectively.

> *He guides the humble in what is right*
> *and teaches them his way.*
>
> ~ Psalm 25:9

> *You guide me with your counsel,*
> *and afterward you will take me into glory.*
>
> ~ Psalm 73:24

> *Guide me in your truth and teach me,*
> *for you are God my Savior.*
>
> ~ Psalm 25: 5

> *For this God is our God for ever and ever;*
> *he will be our guide even to the end.*
>
> ~ Psalm 48:14

> *Teach me, O Lord, to follow your decrees;*
> *then I will keep them to the end.*
>
> ~ Psalm 119:33

No matter how faithful we are, there will always be challenges to deal with in life. And these experiences are times when we can have our most profound Christian growth. Even the strongest Christians have turmoil in their lives! There is only **ONE** time in our lives when everything is peaceful, without any challenges, and that time is **ONLY in heaven!**

I have made decisions that were harmful to my **Spiritual, Physical, Emotional, and Mental Health.** You can substitute your experiences where I have shared two of my examples. There are a variety of ways when we bring UNhealthy situations into our lives. I almost died with **MY CHOICES**, but other choices can be extremely damaging as well. I hope this book helps you to start seeing yourself and your **SPEM Health**, more clearly!

I think you are realizing that being a good Christian does NOT automatically stop ALL your suffering. Life's difficult experiences will ALWAYS be a part of your life on earth so you CAN learn and grow into the person God created you to be. We will always face challenging times; however, thanks to being strengthened by them, we can live more peacefully, no matter what circumstances we face in the future. This is the ongoing building of strength that comes to Christian believers.

As your Christian faith grows, **YOU** will start reaching out to **HELP OTHERS** travel on **THEIR Spiritual Journey.** Those whom you know well and care about, strangers in your pathway, and acquaintances in your life are people **YOU** can reach out to and offer your growing Christian understandings and support. **YOU** can move forward fearlessly, talking about **YOUR** decision to **IMPROVE your SPEM Health.** And, someday, this will become a catchphrase → **"How's your SPEM Health?"**

You can tell people that ups and downs will always be a part of their lives; however, we have a forgiving God. Once they ask for forgiveness of their sins, their slate is wiped clean and no longer remembered by God.

God will be with you every step of the way, guiding you in your Christian approach to help others! You will sense meaningful ways to encourage others to open up about their individual journeys in life. This will give them an opportunity to see themselves more clearly while growing in their closeness to God Almighty.

Praise be to the Lord, for he has heard my cry for mercy.
The Lord is my strength and my shield;
my heart trusts in him, and I am helped.
My heart leaps for joy
and I will give thanks to him in song.

~ Psalm 28:6–7

For God did not appoint us to suffer wrath
but to receive salvation through our
Lord Jesus Christ. He died for us so that,
whether we are awake or asleep,
we may live together with him.
Therefore encourage one another and
build each other up, just as in fact you are doing.

~ 1 Thessalonians 5:9–11

If I had cherished sin in my heart,
the Lord would not have listened;
but God has surely listened and heard my voice in prayer.
Praise be to God, who has not rejected
my prayer or withheld his love from me!

~ Psalm 66:18–20

Although I was raised in a Christian home, my belief in Christ as my Savior did not get much further than thinking my prayers were the foundation of my Christianity. But being a solid Christian takes on much more than ONLY praying about our lives. Thankfully, I now realize that prayers are only one part of being a faithful Christian in God's eyes. I must show God that I am following His will by reading His word, spending time in church to be around other believers, and making wise choices for my **Spiritual, Physical, Emotional, and Mental** good health.

Today, as a faithful servant, I contemplate, **WWJD—What Would Jesus Do?** as I search for better understandings of: what to say, when to say it, where to go, what to do, and how to do things in my life. And, when the day comes that God calls me home, I pray for Him to grant me eternal rest in heaven! **AMEN**

Therefore you do not lack any spiritual gift as you eagerly wait for our Lord Jesus Christ to be revealed. He will keep you strong to the end, so that you will be blameless on the day of our Lord Jesus Christ. God, who has called you

into fellowship with his Son Jesus
Christ our Lord, is faithful.

~ 1 Corinthians 1:7–9

A generous man will prosper; he who refreshes
others will himself be refreshed.

~ Proverbs 11:25

Praise be to the God and Father of our
Lord Jesus Christ, the Father of
compassion and the God of all comfort,
who comforts us in all our troubles,
so that we can comfort those in any trouble
with the comfort we ourselves have received from God.

~ 2 Corinthians 1:3–4

But in your hearts set apart Christ as Lord.
Always be prepared to give answer
to everyone who asks you to give the
reason for the hope that you have.
But do this with gentleness and respect,
keeping a clear conscience,
so that those who speak maliciously against
your good behavior in Christ

may be ashamed of their slander.
It is better, if it is God's will,
to suffer for doing good than for doing evil.
For Christ died for sins once for all,
the righteous for the unrighteous, to bring you to God.
~ 1 Peter 3:15–18

Therefore, if anyone is in Christ he is a new creation;
the old has gone, the new has come!
~ 2 Corinthians 5:17

Trust in the Lord with all your heart and
lean not on your own understanding;
in all your ways acknowledge him, and
he will make your paths straight.
Do not be wise in your own eyes;
fear the Lord and shun evil.
This will bring health to your body and
nourishment to your bones.
~ Proverbs 3:5–8

I can do everything through him who gives me strength.
~ Philippians 4:13

As I stated earlier, after my (2nd) traumatic car accident, I knew what it was like to have my mind/body/spirit foundation dismantled by my personal choices. If I had taken more time to develop a healthier attitude, a better coping structure, improved methods of entertaining myself, and a stronger realization of how to build my present and future life, I might have been able to bypass injuring myself so terribly and causing others to worry so deeply about me, while disappointing God so greatly. I should have spent more time helping my **SPEM Health** to grow in valuable ways. Instead, I chose to ignore my **Spiritual growth,** and I had no respect for my **Physical Health,** while my **Emotional and Mental Health** were stunted due to my irresponsible, stubborn attitude about making **Healthy,** needed changes in my thinking and in my actions.

Therefore, prepare your minds for action;
be self-controlled; set your hope fully on the grace
to be given you when Jesus Christ is revealed.
As obedient children, do not conform to the
evil desires you had when you lived in ignorance.
But just as he who called you is holy, so be holy in all you do;
for it is written: "Be holy, because I am holy."
~ 1 Peter 1:13–16

Yes, God gives us free will to make our own decisions on earth during the hundreds of choices we make every day of our lives, such as, what we say, how we say it, what we do, how we do it, where we go, why we do things, etc. But, as we face decisions, small and large, minor and serious, we do NOT always question the Holy Spirit living within us about the best choices to make. **INSTEAD,** we **ONLY** rely on our ability to make decisions based on our knowledge, feelings, personal agendas, misguided understandings, happiness, hopes, fears, and anger, all of which can improperly influence our decisions. This occurs **WITHOUT** God's guidance being first and foremost in the mix! We need to realize that it is He who knows what is always in our BEST interest. We need to ask God to guide us during our lives on earth. He sees the entire picture of our lives, we do not! So, we need to base our decisions on God's will.

Opening myself to listening to God's will could have been accomplished by, first, nudging (not ignoring) my feelings out of my thoughts, thus quieting the busyness of my mind, while being receptive for the Holy Spirit to "speak" to me. I never hear an actual voice, but, I realize a deep peace flowing within me as I recognize the better decision to make. If you feel UNcomfort-able with a **CHOICE** you are leaning toward, realize the UNeasiness is being brought on by the Holy Spirit within. That is one way God leads us to understand what is in our **BEST INTEREST**, which is His will for our lives. The small voice (feeling) within is the Holy Spirit talking with you.

Had I chosen to listen to the Holy Spirit earlier in time, I would have had opportunities to improve my life! Instead, I stayed on the same downward spiral that I had been traveling on! How hurtful this was to God! After all, He created me, He gave life to me, and He knows what my purpose on earth is! I was acting like I did not matter to myself, or to God, at all!

Today, I freely acknowledge that I am better off leaning on God's will for my decisions on earth. I tried to run my own life for many years but now I absolutely prefer His choices over mine! After all, Father knows best! I pray that you learn to recognize this huge truth in your life, too!

We all, like sheep, have gone astray,
each of us has turned to his own way;

and the Lord has laid on him the iniquity of us all.

~ Isaiah 53:6

I seek you with all my heart;
do not let me stray from your commands.
I have hidden your word in my heart
that I might not sin against you.

~ Psalm 119:10–11

Set your minds on things above, not on earthly things.

~ Colossians 3:2

As I return to my explanation of how God got my attention, please keep in mind that while you will not necessarily have the same type of problems in your life as I had, please develop **YOUR PERSONAL** understanding of how **YOU** are mistreating yourself and how God is reaching out to get your attention about it. I urge you to use my examples to verify what is going on in your life and to help you realize that **YOU CAN IMPROVE** the **CHOICES** you make concerning your **Spiritual, Physical, Emotional, and Mental Health.** That is the essence of this book, **Achieving SPEM Health**™, to help people recognize **THEIR** ability to find and retain **good SPEM Health.**

h.) Four Important Goals to Focus On

Here are four factors that will help you deal more effectively with yourself and others during your life on earth.

Goal #1: Communicate honestly with God, others, and yourself, at all times.

God expects us to be honest at all times. As we share our thoughts and feelings with God, it brings us closer to Him! Even though God knows what we are thinking and feeling before we do, He wants us to become aware of our true inner selves as we discuss what is in our minds and hearts with Him. Hiding our truths causes a distance to come between God and ourselves while stifling our ability to grow properly.

> _Nothing in all creation is hidden from_
> _God's sight. Everything is uncovered_
> _and laid bare before the eyes of him_
> _to whom we must give account._
> ~ Hebrews 4:13

Always, being honest with God, others, and ourselves frees us from the pain and anguish that typically surround lies. Those who choose NOT to be honest suffer greatly as THEIR lies come back to haunt them quickly, and/or, in the future!

NOT being honest ruins an individual's ability to communicate effectively with themselves and others during life experiences. Once you are labeled a liar, no matter how much you are forgiven by your peers, they will not forget when you chose to lie to them. The hurt that develops for those lied to is often tied with the realization that they personally do not lie, and for that reason, did not expect someone to lie to them. They feel needlessly duped and taken advantage of!

It is smart to remember, if someone lies to you, there is **NO** righteousness in choosing to lie to them in return. Two wrongs do NOT make a right!

Do not repay evil with evil or insult with insult,
but with blessing, because to this
you were called so that you may inherit a blessing.
For, "Whoever would love life and see good days
must keep his tongue from evil
and his lips from deceitful speech.

He must turn from evil and do good;
he must seek peace and pursue it.
For the eyes of the Lord are on the righteous
and his ears are attentive to their prayer,
but the face of the Lord
is against those who do evil."

~ 2 Peter 3:9–12

Yes, people **DO** forgive others for their mistakes, but **CHOOSING to LIE** is more than just a simple mistake. It is a conscious act perpetrated by someone who wants to control other human beings, instead of working to understand, improve, and present their thoughts and emotions in a mature, appropriate manner.

Communicating honestly with God, others, and ourselves allows us to stand on solid ground as we experience a wide range of Emotions during everyday situations. Emotions are NOT right or wrong, but how we ACT on our Emotions can be! Therefore, we need to understand where our Emotions are coming from and how to EXPRESS them in healthy ways.

Keep in mind that **YOUR LIES** will damage YOUR perception of YOURSELF, and of OTHERS and of LIFE in general, in a **NEGATIVE MANNER!**

Therefore, do NOT let lies compound the natural effect of tough times in your life. Lies have NO good value and only WORSEN situations. In fact, many things will go awry once **YOU CHOOSE** to **NOT** tell the truth. Staying true to God, others, and yourself, helps you to find more peace in your life!

Goal #2: _Treat others fairly by becoming mindful of how you Emotionally interact with them._

No matter what we are experiencing, we need to make sure that we are NOT displacing our Emotions inappropriately.

I will give the example of anger because it is one of the more difficult Emotions to manage properly. In fact, MANY people do NOT deal with their Emotional upsets in healthy ways. Often, they transfer their anger from a previous situation to a future situation, which was not the original cause of that Emotion.

Transferring anger improperly causes a multitude of problems to occur for ourselves and others. The anger originally felt had not been examined, understood, nor dealt with properly. It was totally ignored, stuffed, and/or, made light of; thus, the feeling of anger later manifests itself improperly during future innocent situations toward innocent people. It is often disguised to others as an Emotion aimed appropriately, but it is NOT!

> *A man of knowledge uses words with restraint,*
> *and a man of understanding is even-tempered.*
>
> ~ Proverbs 17:27

By NOT working to understand WHY we are feeling an Emotion, such as anger, we are unaware of where the Emotion is coming from and how to deal with it properly. However, once you are in touch with your inner self and become mindful of how you interact with yourself AND others, YOU WILL become BETTER at controlling when and how you express your Emotions, including anger!

I explained how anger can become a misdirected emotion because it is an emotion that often inappropriately hurts others. But, there are other Emotions, such as: sadness, envy, fear, guilt, jealousy, anxiousness, frustration, and bitterness. Any of these Emotions, and others, can be misunderstood and expressed inappropriately, which leads to creating difficulties that, otherwise, would not exist.

Goal #3: _Do whatever is necessary to get through demanding situations in the healthiest ways possible._

We get involved in a variety of situations caused either by our own choices or by other people's decisions which have strong influences on us. If we stay open and deal with these times in healthy, practical ways, we can lessen the impact of problematic times and be able to heal complex situations more easily.

God wants us to go through our life on earth by leaning on His words for guidance. Pray for His wisdom to become known to you as you face important decisions.

> _Trust in the Lord with all your heart_
> _and lean not on your own understanding;_
> _in all your ways acknowledge him,_
> _and he will make your paths straight._
>
> ~ Proverbs 3:5–6

But I trust in you, O Lord; I say,
"You are my God." My times are in your
hands; deliver me from my enemies and
from those who pursue me.

~ Psalm 31:14–15

Think back to times when you were on the fringe of another person's difficult experience and could see the hardship they were facing. Did you feel an enormous desire to help them with their problem? I hope you did! Being interested in helping others is God working through YOU to share the messages/lessons and miracles He has for THEM, as He guides YOU in spreading His Word!

God fully understands that, at times, we will be inconvenienced, to one degree or another, as we reach out to help others in need. But, we do NOT want to completely resolve things for others. Instead, we need to help them learn how to get through difficult times as they grow during their experiences. Yes, God wants us to be wise and perceptive of opportunities when we can help to lighten someone else's load. Our kind effort can be of substantial benefit to those we interact with in life. Plus, while we are busy helping someone with their troubles, we often become less focused on our own! It becomes a winning situation for everyone!

What goes around comes around! There is no doubt that what YOU give to others in positive, helpful ways, will come back to YOU tenfold on a day when YOU are in need and, at times, when YOU least expect it to happen! Yes! God works in mysterious ways!

__Goal #4__: Endeavor to learn God's messages within the experiences that you have on earth, while seeing these times as your eternal gateway to heaven.

Everything we experience on earth is meant to prepare us for our eternal life in heaven with God. While on earth, He has a master plan for each of our lives! Following His will is the best way to get the most out of the steady stream of messages He sends our way! These messages are lessons to help guide us as we learn and grow into the person God created us to be.

I will instruct you and teach you in the way you should go;
I will counsel you and watch over you.

~ Psalm 32:8

The Lord will guide you always; he will satisfy your needs.

~ Isaiah 58:11

Remember, you will keep getting the same message in various forms until God realizes that you **VALUE** what you have **LEARNED** and are **READY** for the **NEXT** message. The same truth applies to the message after that one and the next one, and so on. No matter what turmoil enters your life, God will never give you any more than you can manage! It is a lifelong learning process that helps us to grow and mature as we follow His will.

God's messages keep coming to us until the day that He decides to bring us home to be with Him in heaven, a wonderful place where there is NO sorrow, pain, or discomfort! Until then, **NEVER** give up on becoming whom you were meant to be!

In his heart a man plans his course,
but the Lord determines his steps.

~ Proverbs 16:9

Therefore we do not lose heart. Though outwardly
we are wasting away, yet inwardly
we are being renewed day by day.
For our light and momentary troubles
are achieving for us an eternal glory
that far outweighs them all.
So we fix our eyes not on what is seen,
but on what is unseen.
For what is seen is temporary,
but what is unseen is eternal.

~ 2 Corinthians 4:16–18

i.) Personal Efforts and Counseling Work Together

Achieving SPEM Health™ is an incentive to understand and improve your personal thoughts, feelings, actions, and reactions, which will lead you to make better choices in your life. This will allow you to develop a calmer, steadier, less upsetting, healthier lifestyle.

At the point in time when I realized that MY decisions were causing problems to occur in my life, I could not sink any lower! I truly felt burdened by the notion that I was the actual cause for significant problems coming into my life!

Although I was of Christian belief, I was not in tune with God's Word, nor with how He wanted me to live my life. My parents, though loving, did not lead me to find my purpose in life. I made decisions primarily on my own and got involved with others who were drinking alcohol, getting high on pot, smoking cigarettes, and shooting pool. What poor choices I made in my life! Being closer to God's word could have helped steer me in a much better direction!

I had no thoughts about my future, such as: What direction was I working toward in commissioned sales to support myself in the future? Should I pursue a college education to find a better, different direction? How should I spend my free time? What hobbies could I immerse myself in for pleasure?

I was lost and only living one day at a time! It was such an irrational way to exist!

The time came when God helped open my eyes in ways that saved my life. After two traumatic, life-threatening car accidents, I finally came to my senses and realized that I had it wrong, ALL wrong! My life is not my own. It belongs to God! He is my Father, my Creator! Yes, He gave all human beings FREE will on earth, but He wants us to **CHOOSE** to follow His will so we can become the individuals He created us to be. MY personal honesty about MY UNhealthy thoughts AND actions eventually got me started on **My SPEM Health Journey**. Being HONEST with yourself about YOUR misguided CHOICES will help YOU to get started on **Your SPEM Health Journey**! Just never, ever, ever, give up! **YOU CAN DO IT!**

Cast your cares on the Lord and he will sustain you;
he will never let the righteous fall.

~ Psalm 55:22

Do not be anxious about anything,
but in everything, by prayer and petition,
with thanksgiving, present your requests to God.

~ Philippians 4:6

When I finally accepted that I could no longer ignore my responsibility to lead a healthier lifestyle, I understood that it was up to me to start the process of change. Therefore, I started to employ every resource possible toward improving my present and future paths in life. It would have been a godsend if **Achieving SPEM Health**™ would have been on the bookshelves at that time in my life! Having that type of helpful support to improve my **Spiritual, Physical, Emotional, and Mental Health** would have been an enormous help!

In addition to relying on myself and God to understand the reasons behind the obvious POOR choices I had been making, I stopped drinking, smoking pot, and staying up into the early morning hours. I decided to, also, engage in cognitive therapy with a social worker/counselor to unravel what was going on inside my mind and heart. That important decision helped me to gain additional knowledge about my inner thoughts and feelings, which had been foreign to me. Thankfully, I was able to form a deeper psychological perception of how and why I was causing my own pains. This was incredibly freeing for me! I will go back for a **"Mental tune-up"** in an instant if I ever get caught up, again, with situations in life that are UNmanageable, and/or, OVERwhelming!

I continue to counsel myself wisely so my life stays free of UNnecessary difficulties caused by UNhealthy habits, and to avoid new ones. UNhealthy habits have one thing in common: they injure YOU and do NOT support a healthy life. I am proud to no longer ignore my thoughts and feelings and merely EXIST through life. I now deal with difficulties head-on, and I can deal more effectively with problematic life situations. Are all my decisions the best ones to make? **NOPE!** But, I no longer make choices that are as UNhealthy as they were in the past!

Working on your own, and/or, finding a clergyperson, social worker/counselor, or psychologist to help redefine your thoughts and feelings is a great help. Some of you might need a psychiatrist to recommend appropriate medicine to help with mental disorders that have been standing in your way of living a healthier life.

Finding help that we need **IS THE BEST THING TO DO!** Whichever way you choose, it is important to get started on **YOUR** personal journey to help yourself! And, **NEVER** give up improving yourself throughout your life!

When you are in a professional counseling setting, as well as, when you counsel yourself, make sure you **ALLOW** yourself to be counseled! And, be **HONEST** at all times. If you are going to gain deeply from your counseling sessions, it is imperative that you do so.

When you are with a therapist, instead of trying to figure out why you are being asked a question, or what a certain look meant, or inventing false things to say for fear of repercussions, do what I did, and give yourself permission to **TRUST** your counselor and **ALLOW** that person to work **WITH** you. This will help you to speak truthfully and get to know your true inner self more easily. Do NOT sit there and think they will TELL YOU what to do. GOOD Therapists will HELP YOU determine the best way for YOU to **HELP YOURSELF!**

Once you get an understanding of how you have been maneuvering your senses to manipulate your life and the lives of others, you will grow stronger and be able to let go of UNhealthy thoughts and habits. Then, you can replace them with healthier ways of thinking and living. Having friends and family members to talk with can be comforting, but it will NOT be as helpful as talking with a qualified therapist, who is being paid to work on what is in **YOUR BEST INTEREST!** They are trained to ONLY think about YOU and YOUR LIFE. And, keep in mind that, most personal health insurances include a number of counseling sessions paid for in-part, or in-full, per year. Call your health care insurance company to find out! Do **NOT** put this task off. **DO IT NOW!** Then, you can rely on that knowledge for future use, if needed.

Achieving SPEM Health™ is a needed component to engage your thinking in ways that will improve your mind/body/spirit foundation. Think of this book as a starting point from which to work as you dedicate yourself to improving your **SPEM Health and → YOUR life on earth!**

j.) Drugs, Alcohol, Cigarettes, and Other UNhealthy Habits

As I mentioned, time went on and I continued to search deeply into my thinking process to determine what was standing in my way of making better choices in life. I tossed my thoughts and feelings back and forth during **EMOTIONAL** battles within my mind and heart, as I struggled to stay honest about past experiences that contributed to forming my UNhealthy behaviors.

Emotions that are not understood, feelings and thoughts that are not adequately dealt with, and reasonable human needs that are not properly examined nor pursued effectively can each become deadly instruments within the human psyche. This results in the establishment of **UNhealthy habits** that are inappropriately clung to for support throughout life. Therefore, again, we must find ways to counsel ourselves, and/or, find a qualified therapist whenever we are at odds with any part of our **SPEM Health**.

I used drugs, alcohol, and cigarettes while pointlessly escaping from being able to see myself clearly. Thus, **MY CHOICES** sheltered me from comprehending the need to challenge myself to grow and change.

Eventually, I realized that I was using **UNhealthy CHOICES** to live in ways that I thought were perfectly fine because they made me feel good! How sad that I did not realize the short and long term painful consequences that I was causing for myself! The same reasoning is true with many other types of UNhealthy habits that people immerse themselves in as they run from the realities of their life!

UNhealthy choices mask **EMOTIONAL** pains that we need to deal with to live a SENSIBLE, healthy lifestyle. Trust me, learning how to recognize what you need to change about your behavior will eventually help to eliminate many problems from coming into your life. Becoming aware of better ways to manage your **EMOTIONS** will set off enormous healthy changes in how you live your life on earth!

Hindsight absolutely shows how reckless I was living! I did not take time to realize that **MY CHOICES** were extremely disrespectful to God and UNmistakably hurtful to myself. My lifestyle kept me stuck in a daily rut of going nowhere! It may sound trivial to you, but I can remember many times when I sat down, drank a beer, and/or, smoked pot, and/or, a cigarette while I just **THOUGHT** about doing things differently in my life. But I **NEVER** formed any concrete decisions concerning the types of changes I needed to make. Deep down, I knew I was hurting, but I was firmly stuck in the UNhealthy mindset of NOT attempting to understand and improve myself in any way whatsoever! NOT making a decision while doing **NOTHING** different at all is actually making a very UNhealthy decision! **NOT SMART!**

After much prayer and becoming closer to God, I finally started to get serious about **CHANGES** that I needed to make. I prayed to see myself more clearly so I could understand how and why to adjust MY actions and reactions, which had gotten me through life in such an UNproductive, UNhealthy fashion! I wanted to find MY PURPOSE in life and have a better direction to follow! I needed to discipline myself daily if I was going to achieve realistic improvements to my mind/body/spirit health. Does that type of thinking → **APPLY TO YOU, TOO?**

Our fathers disciplined us for a little while
as they thought best; but God disciplines us for our good,
that we may share in his holiness.
No discipline seems pleasant at the time, but painful.

Later on, however, it produces a harvest
of righteousness and peace
for those who have been trained by it.

~ Hebrews 12:10–11

Commit to the Lord whatever you do,
and your plans will succeed.

~ Proverbs 16:3

If the Lord delights in a man's way,
he makes his steps firm;
though he stumble, he will not fall,
for the Lord upholds him with his hand.

~ Psalm 37:23–24

I love my parents dearly, who each passed away years ago. I recognize they did the best they could in raising their children, as many parents do. However, I was fortunate to start understanding what was missing in my life. I could see that because of my own imperfections, I needed stronger parental support and guidance. I, also, needed faithful friends, not those who lived under the same senselessness as I did, only wanting to party, have fun, and ignore the realities of life! I needed to gain a deeper respect and relationship with God and His Word. He KNEW what was missing in my life and which lessons would help me to grow properly. I needed to fully understand my feelings and deal with them effectively, as well as, becoming aware of the direction my thoughts and choices were taking me.

THINK ABOUT IT! What in YOUR past contributes to YOUR defensive behavior of running away from YOUR true self? What is missing in YOUR life that YOU need? Some of YOUR situations probably revolve around different types of UNhealthy circumstances than I experienced. However, they still revolve around similar causes, including how you feel about yourself, and another major one is lack of fulfillment within. Something is missing—it hurts, and we often compensate for it in UNhealthy ways.

As you have read, I worked hard to decipher the **EMOTIONAL** UNtruths that I allowed to guide me inappropriately. My **TRUE** feelings were UNknown to me at that time; therefore, I knew it was going to be challenging work, but, it was a **BETTER CHOICE** than living an UNproductive, UNhealthy, DIFFICULT life! I pray that you will develop a similar determination

to get to know your TRUE self! Your goal will be →
BETTER DAYS AHEAD!

I think people, in general, fear change because they are afraid of the work involved to reach their goals. *Does that sentence describe you?* Do not fear because once you start, small improvements will come along and you will gain a better, healthier perspective about yourself AND your overall life! Then, you can eagerly strive to reach **NEW Healthy goals** that will bring added **PEACE** into your life.

Believe me, YOUR hard work will make YOUR journey in life much easier! **Achieving SPEM Health** will be a REWARD for your efforts! But it is up to YOU to get started on **Your SPEM Health Journey!**

k.) I Could No Longer Just Sit
There and Do Nothing

As I stated earlier, one of the important changes for me in life was to finally stop smoking cigarettes, a physical and psychological addiction. Being successful in reaching that goal, after many years of choosing to have such a harmful, nasty, expensive habit, showed me, even more so, that I could no longer just sit there and do nothing in life! Reaching my decision to STOP that UNhealthy habit was excellent proof that I could continue making smart decisions! **HOW EXCITING!** I truly felt in better control of HOW I was living my life. I knew that God was pleased with my efforts. I could feel His grace pouring into my life!

He has delivered us from such a deadly peril,
and he will deliver us.
On him we have set our hope that
he will continue to deliver us,
as you help us by your prayers.
Then many will give thanks on our behalf
for the gracious favor granted us
in answer to the prayers of many.
Now this is our boast: Our conscience testifies

that we have conducted ourselves in the world,
and especially in our relations with you,
in the holiness and sincerity that are from God.
We have done so not according to worldly wisdom
but according to God's grace.

~ 2 Corinthians 1:10–12

There are **MANY** types of UNhealthy behaviors and habits that people form, which stem from the UNhealthy ways they see themselves and their lives. Being addicted to any type of UNhealthy behavior causes us to run away from our TRUE selves while detrimentally affecting our relationship with God and those around us. In addition to abusing drugs, alcohol, and cigarettes, there are other troubling behaviors that people utilize while ignoring their TRUE selves. Controlling attitudes, verbal abuse, egotistical behavior, immaturity, rudeness, thievery, callousness, physical abuse, dishonesty, laziness, emotional abuse, and irresponsibility are some of them. You are probably familiar with others that can be added to the list!

As you read **Achieving SPEM Health**™ and feel more comfortable to start making needed changes to improve your mind/body/spirit health, you will develop a better attitude about yourself and life in general. You will stop being burdened with UNresolved issues that interfere with YOUR ability to treat yourself and others fairly in life. Your growth will be part of forming your wisdom! **HOW GREAT!**

Blessed is the man who finds wisdom;
the man who gains understanding.

~ Proverbs 3:13

You truly need to recognize **YOUR UNhealthy** behaviors. You know them best! You are living with them! But, after making the smart choice to get started on your own, and/or, with counseling to see yourself more clearly and learn how AND why to stop UNhealthy habits, **BE PREPARED** for some troubling times to crop up during the FIRST steps involved with your decision. The damaging patterns you had been living with that brought pain and disappointment into your life, will try to emerge again! These controlling habits that established UNhealthy ways that helped you through life, will surely raise their evil heads repeatedly trying to get your attention **AGAIN!** You **MUST** become stronger than you were in the past when **YOU allowed** those evil, disruptive behaviors to become a part of your life! The devil enjoys strengthening people's weaknesses! **NOT GOOD!** So, stand **STRONG** while you grow to reach your new, **SPEM Healthy Goals!**

Submit yourselves, then to God.
Resist the devil, and he will flee from you.

~ James 4:7

Like a city whose walls are broken down
is a man who lacks self-control.

~ Proverbs 25:28

Be self-controlled and alert.
Your enemy the devil prowls around
like a roaring lion looking for someone to devour.
Resist him, standing firm in the faith,
because you know that your brothers
throughout the world are undergoing
the same kind of sufferings.

~ 1 Peter 5:8–9

Do **NOT** worry. As time goes on, you will eventually realize that YOU are in control of YOUR thoughts AND actions! You will NO longer flee from the responsibility to see yourself more clearly. You will live your life in a **HEALTHIER** manner while growing into the person God created you to be! YOU ARE making the **BEST** decision of your life to replace your UNhealthy habits with **HEALTHY** ones! Stand strong and never let the past evil temptations have power in your life ever again! And YES, not long from now, you will be on your way to a happier, more productive, healthier lifestyle with fewer problems! This reasoning worked for me, and I know it can work for you!

Remember, God will be joyful that you have become wiser about living your life to the fullest, healthiest extent possible on earth! And, remember, **NEVER GIVING UP** is a necessary component in reaching your goals more quickly!

Dear friend, I pray that you may enjoy good health and that all may go well with you, even as your soul is getting along well.

~ 3 John 2

1.) Get Started by Taking Responsibility for Your Life

We all know that recognition is 90% of the solution to the problem! As we become aware of how to improve our lives and steadily move forward in a healthy, productive manner, we are helping ourselves and improving our relationship with God! Ignoring the precious miracle of our birth is extremely UNjust and does NOT please Him. We must show greater respect for our **SPEM Health, our life, and for God!**

But just as he who called you is holy, so be holy in all you do; for it is written: "Be holy, because I am holy."
~ 1 Peter 1:15–16

No one else is accountable for OUR choices in life; therefore, WE must take responsibility for how we think AND act. Yet, often, people of all ages continue to blame their parents for what their life is like today! Is that what you are doing? If so, keep in mind that no matter which biological or adoptive parent(s) raised you, or if you were orphaned, no matter what type of upbringing you had, you MUST take responsibility for YOUR own life sooner, rather than later!

Remember, it does NOT matter what happens to YOU in life, it is how YOU handle it that counts! What an important statement! The longer you take to end the blame you harbor within your mind and heart against anyone for what happened in your past, the longer your life will be filled with difficult, insurmountable problems! You MUST learn to take responsibility for YOUR life, fix what you can, accept the rest, and move on, as you realize that NOBODY lives a life without any turmoil. There are different types of ups-and-downs in every person's life on earth!

You can be certain that resentment and bitterness will surely inhibit your **Healthy mind/body/spirit growth!** Therefore, start your healing process by forgiving those who have hurt you, including yourself! As time moves on, your life will fill up with many "happy" experiences that will leave less room for the "hurtful ones." In other words, your thought processes will "even out" as you relish making happy memories! For anyone who has been hurt in ways that are UNbearable, and/or, legally UNcalled for, please contact therapists to help you sort things out, AND, when needed, please call the proper authorities who can help in seeking justice for the person, and/or, people involved who harmed you.

We need to forgive those who have brought pain into our lives so we can lessen the hold those painful memories have on ourselves and our lives. But, evil people **MUST** be held accountable for their improper actions. And remember, **YOU** are **NOT** expected to struggle on your own with those types of memories. Get the help you need! **AMEN**

> *For if you forgive men when they sin*
> *against you, your heavenly Father*
> *will also forgive you.*
> *But if you do not forgive men their sins,*
> *your Father will not forgive your sins.*
>
> ~ Matthew 6:14–15

Use this wonderful Prayer, mentioned in the Introduction, as you move forward in your quest to take responsibility for your life. It was an enormous help to me, and I still live by it! **"Serenity Prayer"→ "God, grant me the Serenity to accept the things I cannot change, Courage to change the things I can, and the Wisdom to know the difference!"** Stay true to this prayer and it will be a big help throughout your entire life!

Stay open to acknowledging what you are doing that interferes with being able to go through your days and nights with less struggle. To succeed in your journey to find and retain good **Spiritual, Physical, Emotional, and Mental Health,** you must find the strength to **HOLD YOURSELF RESPONSIBLE** for YOUR personal actions AND non-actions of yesterday, today, AND tomorrow! NOT doing so about yesterday will keep you stuck in the past! NOT doing so for today will immobilize you now! And NOT doing so concerning tomorrow eliminates any chance for you to have a healthier, stress-free future! If there are people in your life who are negative influences, then stay away from them! ONLY choose to be around people who are positive influences! Remember → **IT'S UP TO YOU!**

Believe in your ability to become your own BEST advocate on earth! As you set out to examine your past, present, and future experiences, do what you need to do to avoid various pitfalls that can occur during your journey. But if they occur, do not let those times concern you. Keep believing and advocating for yourself of your right to make improvements in your life! And remember, ups and downs ALWAYS surround one's growth! Do **NOT** become fearful and ONLY think about →

YOUR BACKSLIDES. Instead, travel through your steps of growth in confidence and with a solid commitment to continue traveling onward and upward! **Learn from any mistakes that arise!** But, NEVER give up striving to reach your goals, or you will miss ALL the GOOD that God has in store for YOU! And remember, tomorrow just may be ➜ **the BEST day of your ENTIRE LIFE!** GO FOR IT with open arms, knowing that statement is true!

Your word is a lamp to my feet and a light for my path.
~ Psalm 119:105

The Lord is my light and my salvation—whom shall I fear?
The Lord is the stronghold of my life—
of whom shall I be afraid?
~ Psalm 27:1

m.) Pray for God's Will to Become Your Will

How do we understand God's will for us? What makes the most sense is to pray for **YOUR WILL** to be molded into **HIS WILL**. In other words, pray for YOUR thoughts and feelings to become more in line with what God wants for you. Pray to make **GOOD** decisions during your days and nights on earth. And continually ask God to help you become successful on your lifelong journey to improve your relationship with Him.

*Anyone who listens to the word but does
not do what it says is like a man
who looks at his face in a mirror and,
after looking at himself, goes away
and immediately forgets what he looks like.*

~ James 1:23–24

As you search for answers to life's perplexing situations, some solutions will be found immediately while others may NEVER seem to come your way. Faithfully accepting the unknown and YOUR limitations, as well as, YOUR successes and unique abilities, makes it possible for YOU to → **LET GO and LET GOD!** When you search for answers that you canNOT decipher, remember it is true that God NEVER gives you more than you can handle!

Stay passionately committed to your journey even through the unknown. Then you will continue to move forward successfully! As time goes on, you WILL find more answers than nonanswers. Plus, you will find NEW opportunities that God is guiding you toward! **HOW EXCITING!** Let Go and Let God for answers not found yet. And have NO FEAR associated with YOUR belief that, ***"With God all things are possible!"*** Move forward in faith while trusting that God will take care of the rest! He always has your BEST interest in mind! One day, you will gratefully say, "I never thought I would be this happy in life!" You will be saying those words due to YOUR proud feeling that can ONLY come from being resilient in your quest for a better life!

> *Trust in the Lord and do good;*
> *dwell in the land and enjoy safe pasture.*
> *Delight yourself in the Lord and he will*
> *give you the desires of your heart.*
> ~ Psalm 37:3–4

Do you realize that God, truly, has specific plans for each of us during our lives! **CAN YOU IMAGINE?** God has a myriad of wonderful ideas, enormous challenges, and beautiful blessings to bestow upon each of us, which, in one way or another, will effectively mold us to become all of who He created us to be on earth! Following His guidance causes us to use our mind/body/spirit resources that He has given to us. Continue to be receptive to His will becoming your will!

Teach me to do your will, for you are my God;
may your good Spirit lead me on level ground.
~ Psalm 143:10

"For I know the plans I have for you," declares the Lord,
"plans to prosper you and not to harm you,
plans to give you hope and a future."
~ Jeremiah 29–11

n.) Everything Is Connected in Life

It often crosses my mind that many things in life connect through a chain of events! **YOUR** choices and decisions, based on **HEALTHY** thoughts, have a better chance of impacting your life AND the lives of others in positive, meaningful ways! As a result, the HEALTHY impact that you have on the lives of others will enable those people to react in HEALTHY ways! Then, their HEALTHY reactions, based on their HEALTHY thoughts, will have a HEALTHY impact on others, and so on, and so forth. What goes around comes around! Can you see this occurring in your life?

Think about a time when someone's HEALTHY behavior impacted you in an appropriate, HEALTHY manner. And also, think about a time when someone's UNhealthy behavior caused **PAIN and HURT** to come into your life. Either way, their choices strongly influenced YOUR reactions and may have caused YOU to treat others in like manners!

It is easy to understand that when a person **CHOOSES** to act in a HEALTHY manner, they do NOT place a burden on the person they interact with so that person is NOT harmed by a HEALTHY communication method. Therefore, that person, in turn, will likely respond in-kind and have HEALTHY connections with those they communicate with afterward.

However, the **FIRST PERSON** in the chain of events who chooses to act in an UNhealthy manner toward another will put an UNhealthy burden on that person to respond in a positive manner. And, the person who received the UNhealthy burden can easily become an injured self and may form UNhealthy habits to deal with the pain they received. Then, that person might pass UNhealthiness, in one form or another, to others whom they interact with, and so on, and so forth.

HEALTHY and **UNhealthy** connections influence people, one-by-one, and eventually, all around the world! Which way do **YOU** want to be responsible for connecting and influencing others? **THINK ABOUT IT!**

I will add that it is absolutely possible for people who ARE hurting to treat themselves and others in a responsible, HEALTHY fashion. Keep in mind that God asks us to treat others as we wish to be treated. So, we NEED to do what we can, daily, to understand ourselves and control our actions and reactions in our life situations. Freeing our minds and hearts from INNER PAINS will allow us to connect with and treat others properly. We can **EACH** have a profound effect on reducing other people's improper behavior by bettering **our OWN** behavior **FIRST** in OUR "little corner of the world!" What you give is what you will eventually get! **THINK ABOUT IT!**

Do to others as you would have them do to you.

~ Luke 6:31

If you really keep the royal law found in Scripture, "Love your neighbor as yourself," you are doing right.

~ James 2:8

o.) Improve Your Outlook on
Yourself and Your Life

Achieving SPEM Health™ recommends that you take care of all four of your **SPEM Health components**. The great results from your effort will be obvious as you stop having turmoil within your inner thoughts and your actions in life. When you recognize these HEALTHY changes in your own life, be sure to give yourself **CREDIT** for being **RESILIENT** and sticking to your **SMART** decision to learn and grow!

Now, you will be able to share your wisdom with others! Tell people about the good that came from adjusting your thoughts, feelings, actions, and reactions. This will encourage others to believe they can do the same thing in THEIR life! God will be speaking through you to others! And referring this book to people you know will give added support to THEIR new **SPEM Health Journey** in life! **WHAT HAVE THEY GOT TO LOSE?** You will be the proof they need, which shows → **IT CAN BE DONE!**

[God] comforts us in all our troubles,
so that we can comfort those in any
trouble with the comfort we ourselves
have received from God.

~ 2 Corinthians 1:4

Each one should use whatever gift he has received
to serve others, faithfully administering
God's grace in its various forms.

~ 1 Peter 4:10

Until God Almighty calls us to be with Him in heaven, He wants us to live our lives on earth to the fullest! Therefore, becoming mindful of your **Spiritual, Physical, Emotional, and Mental Health is ESSENTIAL!** With your mind/body/spirit foundation in the best shape possible, you will TRULY be able to live your life more FULLY! Your efforts to help yourself will result in broadening your appreciation for God's creation of the miraculous state of YOUR being!

No matter what type of mind/body/spirit foundation we are born with, able-bodied, able-minded, or challenged in any way, we need to pay attention to the specific ways in which **WE CAN IMPROVE** our overall health daily! And, no matter what age you are today, or will be tomorrow, each part of our foundation draws from the others to become the entire person that God created us to be! Therefore, our **Spiritual, Physical, Emotional, and Mental Health** is incredibly important, and each part needs to always be well-cared for by us!

> *If one part suffers, every part suffers with it;*
> *if one part is honored, every part rejoices with it.*
> ~ 1 Corinthians 12:26

Achieving SPEM Health is a journey worth taking!

In Closing

Throughout the ups and downs in life, your present and future decisions will help to determine how you feel and in what direction your overall life is headed. What you do with the one life that God has entrusted to your care is up to you! So, **NEVER** give up improving the choices you make, the actions you take, and the reactions you have, to whatever comes into **YOUR LIFE!** Yes, **YOUR LIFE!** Remember, it is **YOU** who is responsible for leading **YOUR LIFE** in the Healthiest direction possible!

Therefore, as you grow closer to God's guidance, re-read, **Achieving SPEM Health**™ to gain helpful support in finding and retaining good **Spiritual, Physical, Emotional, and Mental Health!** The combination will help produce the improved life you have been praying for!

God is pleased that you have decided to take the first steps in the most important decision of your life: to take the best care of the **MIRACLE** that He created → **YOU!**

In GOOD SPEM Health...*always!*

And we pray this in order that you may
live a life worthy of the Lord
and may please him in every way:
bearing fruit in every good work,
growing in the knowledge of God,
being strengthened with all power
according to his glorious might
so that you may have great endurance and patience.

~ Colossians 1:10–11

The END of this book...

...is the BEGINNING of YOUR
HEALTHY transformation!

Thoughtful Guidance for
Your SPEM Health Journey
by, Judith C. Lista

Life is not a dress rehearsal.
Make the adjustments you need in your life, today!

~~~

Face each day in prayer that you will
make it a good productive day,
your objectives will be fulfilled, and you
will have success reaching various goals.
That type of thinking helps your days go by
without negative influences…from you!

~~~

The only way any of us can become our best selves
is by truly being challenged!

~~~

We are each a part of people's growth in life.
In one way or another our interactions
will influence each other's
thoughts, emotions, and behaviors.

Are we going to challenge the
direction of people's growth
in a positive way? Or, in a negative way?
Let's choose a positive way!

~~~

God wants us to learn from our wrongdoings
so we can learn, grow, and go on!
Holding on to unforgiveness will
only limit your growth.
When you ask God for forgiveness,
remember to forgive yourself, too!

~~~

Do what you do best and pray about the rest!

~~~

May your experiences of today,
fulfill your dreams of yesterday!

SPEM Prayers
by, Judith C. Lista

Dear God,

Please forgive me for all my sins,

wrongs, and mistakes.

I have done these things because…

(add specific details here)

Please help me to stop committing these problems

so I no longer hurt you, others, or myself.

AMEN

~~~

Dear God,

Thank you for the many blessings in my life…

(add specific details here)

I don't know where I would be without you.

I want to stay "right" by your side through this life

and through our eternity together!

AMEN

~~~

Dear God,

I pray for everyone I know, everyone I don't know,

everyone I will know, everyone I won't know,

and everyone I have known,

plus, myself and my family, so we are all

Spiritually, Physically, Emotionally, and Mentally

well-balanced and taken care of

until we are each called to be with you in heaven.

AMEN

SPEM Affirmations
by, Judith C. Lista

I am interested in bettering the way I live my life
and the impact I make on others.

~~~

I am a strong advocate for effective communication
during all aspects of my life.

~~~

I know that I decide my own fate
as I make decisions during my lifetime.

~~~

I will continue to be aware of my perceptions
and take responsibility for them as I become more
open and respectful of other people's perceptions.

~~~

I will keep the essence of love
flowing through my life,
for I know that it is only by loving that

I will be able to give of myself fully and that
I will be able to receive from others completely.

~~~

I believe that the past cannot be changed,
but the future can be.
I will not let my mind, body, or soul lie dormant.
I will use every resource I have to
change my future for the better.

~~~

I know that with each experience,
I can learn and grow
no matter how joyful or how
devastating things may seem.

~~~

I vow to look for every hidden meaning during
my experiences from which I can benefit.

~~~

I realize that recognition of a problem is needed
before I can find a solution for it.

~~~

I will speak without offending and
listen without defending.

~~~

I will treat myself and all others by the **R.U.L.E.**
with **R**espect, **U**nderstanding, **L**ove, and **E**quality.

~~~

I cannot feel joy →if
I do not know sorrow.
I cannot feel satisfaction → if
I do not know disappointment.
And, I cannot feel love → if
I do not understand myself.

~~~

I believe that my life will be easier
if I willingly trust myself and
others for guidance. In so doing,
I will be learning throughout the rest of my life.
For I know that if I stop learning,
my life will become more difficult,
and I will no longer be living my life to its fullest.

~~~

I will stop to think, **_What would Jesus do?_** during the many decisions that I need to make throughout my lifetime!

Take Notes on Your SPEM Health Journey!

Take Notes on Your SPEM Health Journey!

Take Notes on Your SPEM Health Journey!

Take Notes on Your SPEM Health Journey!

Take Notes on Your SPEM Health Journey!

Take Notes on Your SPEM Health Journey!

Take Notes on Your SPEM Health Journey!

Take Notes on Your SPEM Health Journey!

Take Notes on Your SPEM Health Journey!

Take Notes on Your SPEM Health Journey!

Take Notes on Your SPEM Health Journey!

Take Notes on Your SPEM Health Journey!